BULGARIA 1879–1946
THE CHALLENGE OF CHOICE

BY TATIANA KOSTADINOVA

EAST EUROPEAN MONOGRAPHS, BOULDER
DISTRIBUTED BY COLUMBIA UNIVERSITY PRESS, NEW YORK

1995

EAST EUROPEAN MONOGRAPHS, NO. CDXXIX

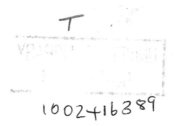

10024-16389

TABLE OF CONTENTS

INTRODUCTION

In the course of my work in the Central State Archives at the beginning of 1988, I came across some interesting data on the parliamentary elections for the Twenty-fifth National Assembly, held in December 1939 – January 1940. The Royal Institute kept deputy candidate lists and the results of the elections. In the margins of the papers a careful police officer had marked the political membership of each of the participants. Further study of these data showed the political passions and dispositions in Bulgarian society in the environment of the non-party regime in 1934.

The paradox was that my discovery came in times when the one-party political system in Bulgaria practiced "elections" with no free choice; when the elections of legislative bodies in this country as a supreme expression of individual choice had become a farce—a skewed "social activity". Results like 99.99% and the lack of actual competition destroyed interest in the event itself. No one in Bulgaria, except the rulers themselves, cared about the results of the elections. No one considered his own participation—his one vote—important for the future development of the country. There were "governmental candidates" back in 1939; fifty years later, during the rule of the Communist party, only government candidates were on the ballot.

This was what provoked my interest in the past political development. There was a time when a certain socio-political practice existed and then it was spoiled and finally abolished. It is the right and the tradition to choose, to feel the challenge and responsibility of that moment when everyone should be permitted to choose according to his conscience; to say: "This is what I believe".

My research was profoundly affected in the days and months following events of the end of 1989, events which shattered Eastern Europe and abolished the wall between it and the democratic world. The final months of my work coincided with the first free parliamentary elections in the country after forty-four years of communist regime. They took place in an environment of multi-party system, freedom of the press and vigorous campaigning by the various parties and candidates.

The lack of independent studies on the election history of Bulgaria corresponded to the insufficient interest in the elections of the society itself.

The very few studies available were almost always dictated by ideological canons and dwelt upon the development of the Electoral Law—the changes in election procedures, the behavior of the political elite, the strategy of the parties in the election process. For obvious reasons most of these studies were about the participation of the Party of "Narrow" socialists, later the Communist Party, in the elections and their achievements. The analyses of the other participants—their partners or opponents were either excluded entirely or were distorted.

The work in this book has been directed to a review of the social and political development of Bulgaria after the Liberation in 1878, and in particular of the political behavior of the parties and the voters. My study encompasses the period between 1879—the time of the adoption of the first Bulgarian Constitution by the Constituent Assembly in Veliko Turnovo—to 1946, when for the last time before the communist regime, voters were given the possibility of choice among political opponents.

The formation and development of the party system are examined in the book in a direct link to the specific clauses in the Electoral Law and its changes made by and in favor of political forces. Very interesting for me was the study of the socio–political activity of the voters—who voted, why and how he or she made their choice, the influence of demographic, ethnic, social and other factors on the voters' behavior, their place of residence and sex. The legacy from the five centuries of foreign domination, in terms of psychology and social behavior, gave cause for interesting observations and conclusions. The lack of sociological studies for the period and the small amount of statistics (many of which were destroyed during the 1950's as being a product of "bourgeois" statistics) prevented the further study of this issue. However, the existing data can paint a realistic picture of the behavior and the motivation of the voters.

The influence of the legacy itself proved to be of significance for taking the decision to participate. The compulsory vote, introduced in 1919, led to an artificially high degree of activity. This is why it is very hard for the present day investigator to establish the real percentage of political participation for the period between the two world wars.

The periodicals and the police reports of the time include assessments, declarations and observations related to the evaluation of the election race by government and by opposition forces. I consider it interesting and useful to trace the hopes and expectations of the political rivals and their responses to the election results. These were sometimes marked with elation, self–contempt, bitterness and often covetousness. The interference of police and administration or their non–presence are also indicators for clarification of the election mechanisms, and are sometimes reasons for unexplainable facts.

The regional peculiarities in the behavior of the voters is one of my main subtopics. Separate regions with recurrent kinds of responses can be seen, sometimes resulting from the level of education, ethnic origin and sometimes from places of birth of the political leaders. Because of the restoration of the original party structures in 1989–1990, it is important to see whether they still have their traditional influence in the different regions. In this respect the victory of the opposition in the elections for the VII Grand National Assembly in June 1990 in the regions where they gained the highest results in the 1946 elections, was very indicative.

I decided to include the two referenda of 1922 and 1946 because these unique events in the history of Bulgaria demonstrate political dispositions and moods; they are not widely known and perhaps of greatest importance, there have recently been discussions favoring proceedings against ministers from former governments, as well as about the legitimacy of the referendum in favor of a republic.

The materials used are taken from the National Library "SS ST Cyril and Methodeus" and the Bulgarian Academy of Sciences—periodicals, the Statistical Yearly of the Kingdom of Bulgaria and the Election Statistics for deputies for National Assemblies; the Central Archives—Royal Institute Fund, National Assembly Fund, Police Department Fund, political function-aries and deputies funds; Ministry of Interior's Archives—reports and files of contributors and district governors, programs and declarations of political parties and coalitions; State Archives (Rousse)—documents for election campaigns and tactics in the region.

The charts and the enclosures after the text recapitulate the official statistical data and illustrate the conclusions of the analyses. Election results in 1884, 1908, 1938, 1939/40 for the different political parties have been established after careful study of archives and periodicals and as such are not published in the statistical information of the Central Statistical Institute.

In terms of methodology, of great help to me were S. Lipset's monograph, "Political Man", and the study "Germany at the Polls". New inspiration and ideas came from talks with Prof. Sirkov, Prof. G. Sartori, Prof. J. Fishkin. The writer Barbara Pomeroy was of great support during the long days of my work on this book, and gave generously of her time and editing skill. I would like sincerely to thank them all.

Tatiana Kostadinova

CHAPTER I
1879-1899—BUILDING OF PARLIAMENTARY POLITICAL SYSTEM

Heritage from the Turkish Domination

The liberation of Bulgaria in 1878 came relatively late; Greece and Serbia already had well-established positions as independent states. The new kingdom of Bulgaria had hardly taken its first breath when it found itself a prisoner of the complex Eastern problem and the entangled selfish interests of the Great Powers. A new state, mindful of its outstanding world presence in the past, was reviving.

It was not until nearly two decades later, toward the end of the nineteenth century that the world began to recognize the "Bulgarian wonder". The rapid leap in the development of the economy, trade, transport, building and communications, based upon local preferences and actively supported by the state, had brought the kingdom to its feet. It began to move forward swiftly and eagerly, striving to catch up with those who had so confidently been striding ahead for a long time.

The Bulgarian politicians, representatives of different national-liberation political trends, quickly moved to establish the first party formations and state institutions, determined to ensure a normal political life for the country. Following the models and traditions established in Europe, they succeeded in reaching their goal, although the rest of the world had expected awkwardness and confusion to prevail.

The political division between "young" and "old" from the revolutionary liberation movement immediately before the Liberation generated the two main lines in Bulgarian political life for decades ahead – the liberal and the conservative. They became clear early in the sessions of the Constituent Assembly, which was convened during the spring of 1879 in the old capital of Turnovo, when the principles of the first Bulgarian Constitution were defended.

The "young" were radical national revolutionists, appealing for a decisive and revolutionary solution of the Bulgarian national problem and realization of the national supreme goal, often called "Bulgaria from San-Stefano". They were relying mainly on the power of the Bulgarian

5

society itself. The "young" were free-thinking and daring and laid the foundation of the liberal political trend, which grew into the Liberal Party.

The "old" were moderates, patriots giving priority to the school and church movement for the revival and education of the Bulgarians on their road to liberty. They relied on help from abroad and were insufficiently convinced of the power of the Bulgarian society to rule itself. They even favored the idea of a dualistic kingdom within the framework of the Ottoman Empire.

These politicians were comparatively well-to-do; most had been educated in Russia. They were more respectable and more cautious, more reasonable and more difficult when it came to making decisions for changes. It was natural for them to establish the conservative trend in Bulgarian political life and later to found the Conservative Party.

These two trends originating in the period of the Bulgarian national revival would determine the direction of Bulgarian political life for decades to come. The generation of politicians who took part in the liberation movement set the foundations of Parliamentary life in the country. It was not by chance that one of their eminent contemporaries, Simeon Radev, called them in his memoirs "creators of contemporary Bulgaria".[1] These men bore some remnants of the past; they were often awkward, impatient and pathetic in their attempt to copy European political customs and behavior. But they were the pioneers who created and passed the Constitution from Tarnovo in 1879 that guaranteed a large number of democratic rights for the Bulgarian people. They created the new state—offices, administration, police and army, finance ministry. Clearly Bulgaria at that time had its politicians, able to establish the foundations of its state system.

The first monarch of Bulgaria was a foreigner with no family roots in the Bulgarian past. He came from Berlin, a twenty-two-year-old lieutenant related to almost all European reigning dynasties at that time; he stayed seven years, then returned to Europe. But he "came back" to Bulgaria after his death and was buried in the center of the capital city of Sofia. His youth and inability to understand the Bulgarian spirit and soul were impediments to a long reign. As an aristocrat he always favored the Conservatives, which gave them the advantage of often having one of their own named Prime Minister. But the common people preferred the "young"—the Liberals. Elitism was foreign to the majority of Bulgarians. That is the reason that the attempt to cancel the Constitution and to establish a regime of the commissions failed and predetermined the fate of Prince Alexander I Battenberg.

The long years of foreign domination left its imprint, particularly on the psychology of the Bulgarian people. They were timid and unsure in their social behavior, they were suspicious and mistrustful, prone to suspicion and disrespectful of the state institutions due to their automatic linking of the institutions with the foreign rule. It is not surprising that the Bulgarians were more independent, more democratic in behavior and initiative only in school, in "*tchitalishte*" (library club) and in church. It was in those places that they were able to communicate using their own language, practice their culture and their faith; there were no foreign institutions or persons belonging to another religion. These were the places, attended by all Bulgarians, where they read the history of their people, sang their songs, held their theatre performances, prayed to "their" God.

It was not like that in political life. At the time when the ordinary Bulgarian could at last freely take part in the social and political life of his state, the enslaving mechanisms of indifference, negligence and even fear were activated again. Thus it was not casual circumstance that after the Liberation even in the beginning of the twentieth century the participation of the Bulgarian electorate in the parliamentary elections was feeble, hardly reaching 50 per cent at best.

It is a fact that there were other valid reasons for this event: pre–election terror; peculiarities in the Electoral Law; disappointment in the political parties and their constant struggle and fierce attacks. There were not polling stations in each settlement and often the peasant had to drop his farm work and go by foot for miles to vote. Nevertheless the main reason for not taking part, and regular non–participation of more than half of those having the right to vote was their persuasion from the past, that the problems would be solved without their participation; that it was more important to ensure their daily bread than to influence the government. Having lived in conditions of foreign domination for five centuries, the Bulgarians did not develop conscientious respect for state institutions. They needed some time to realize that after 1878 it was their country, not the Ottoman Empire, where they lived and where they were given the constitutional right to choose the Government of Bulgaria.

Universal Suffrage

The deputies who took part in the Constituent Assembly in 1879 in the old capital city Turnovo, were determined on three points. According to Article 4 of the Berlin agreement, an assembly should be summoned in the Bulgarian Principality consisting of notables who must pass a Constitution. The Russian Empire commissioner after consulting "different people" made the decision that the Constituent Assembly was to consist of the following groups of representatives: 1. by right (higher clergy and officialdom); 2. by the commissioner's appointment; and 3. by the people's choice (in two stages – the people elected "*glasni*" (delegates), and they elected deputies, in such a way that one deputy was elected to represent 10,000 voters, according to the provisional rules for election of judges.[2] Simeon Radev wrote that there was a fourth group, representing culture societies (for example the "*Napredak*" ("Progress") society in Wien).[3]

Historians and investigators of that period are unanimous that even appointed in this way, the first Bulgarian deputies represented in a proper way the country's post–Liberation society. The Assembly had the necessary representative character to create the most important Law for the new state. This was supported by the fact that the Bulgarian society was properly represented by the presence of East Roumelian deputies in Turnovo.

According to Article 1 of the Election Law, passed with one reading during the last session of the Constituent Assembly, those enfranchised were male, Bulgarian citizens over 21, having civil and political rights as stated in the Constitution, resident in the countryside or in a town, or settled there for at least six months. Eligible candidates (Article 22) were all Bulgarian citizens over 30, having civil and political rights and being literate. The voting (Article 12) would be carried out by secret ballot.[4] The electors were required to bring a "voting–paper" which had already been filled in with as many names as the number of the deputies to be elected in the county, district or town. The "voting–paper" had to be hand–folded, one of the members of the electoral college had to sign it, and the Chairman must put it in the ballot–box. The electors were not obliged by Law to vote.

The implementation of general suffrage with no requirements for educational or property qualifications was a major attribute in the attempt of the new principality even in the beginning of its Parliamentary life to enter the modern world. Only women and foreign citizens had no right to vote.

The lack of substantial restrictions in the status of the electorate gave in practice the opportunity to the entire male population to go to the ballot-boxes. Now, when we evaluate the significance of the general suffrage in Bulgaria as a serious foundation for political democracy in the country, we chance upon another problem. Was the Bulgarian citizen ready to take advantage of this right? Was he mature and well orientated enough to make his choice? The right to vote had already been given. Was it sufficient for the Bulgarians, who had until recently lived under the yoke of the Sultan's Turkey, to accept the challenge?

The lack of traditional political culture would be sensed very soon. According to the Law, Bulgaria had become one of the most democratic states in the world. There was no aristocracy; the prevailing sense, cultivated during the years of oppressive Ottoman rule, was that of equal belonging to the Christian population in the Empire. Thus, the arranging of general suffrage by law turned out to be easy because it was in harmony with the Bulgarian mentality and morality. It was far more difficult to bring to life the functioning of the Parliamentary mechanism, already achieved in many European states. Only the Conservatives (the "Olds") worried about that and insisted on the introduction of electoral qualification and a bicameral chamber. However, the liberally disposed deputies kept the Conservative vote weak at the Constituent Assembly sessions.

The changes made in the Election Law in 1880, were aimed at bringing to a minimum the attempts to take advantage of the legislature to benefit state employees. Deprived of the right to be elected were members of the military, state employees (excluding the ministers), persons with clerical rank and those who had agreements with the government for providing supplies. These changes improved the Election Law and guaranteed the separation of legislative from executive power. New changes in the Election Law were prepared and inaugurated by the Monarch and the Conservatives in the summer of 1882, during the so-called "Regime of the Commissions".

The elections for the First and the Second National Assembly which were held on September 30, 1879 and January 20, 1880 were a total triumph for the Liberals.[5] Despite strongly suspected violations of the law in Gabrovo, Rousse, Trun, etc. the electorate voted resolutely in favor of the liberal candidates. Out of 170 deputies elected to the First National Assembly, only 30 backed the conservative Government. In the Second National Assembly, the Liberals maintained a marked superiority.

Because of these events, Prince Battenberg and the conservative politicians introduced what was to them the only suitable voting system—a two-stage system by which voting was not direct, but through elected delegates. Support for this could be found in the practice of the times. On the first date of the elections only a few voters came to the ballot-boxes and the elections had to be postponed to another date when the future deputies were elected with too few votes. This was particularly a problem in the rural regions where a peasant would hardly leave his work for two days to go to the town to vote.

The Conservatives envisaged too low a number of deputies—only 56. An educational and property qualification was requested, civil servants and teachers could not be elected. The ministers were granted the right to be nominated everywhere.[6] These changes were met with caustic criticism by the Liberals, because it meant that the Government from a body controlled by the Assembly became a body which controlled the Assembly.

The results from the elections of deputies for the Third National Assembly in November, 1882 justified the changes. Out of 56 deputies, 49 were Conservatives, mainly wealthy merchants and rich peasants, 13 of whom were Turks.[7] The political failure of the Monarch's Regime of the Commissions predetermined the fate of the new Election Law. The attempt to establish a two-stage system for elections and bicameral chamber failed due to the ultimate unpopularity of the regime and the innovations of the Conservatives. The failure was due to a large extent to the democratic values of Bulgarian society established during the period of the national Revival.

Advantage to the Liberals

Because of the voting system at the time and the lack of detailed statistics it is very hard today to establish precisely the percentage of influence of the Liberals and the Conservatives in the first post-Liberation years. Nevertheless, it is known that in general, the Liberals were far more popular among the majority of the Bulgarian people.

During the reign of Alexander I Battenberg (not a contradiction to the Constitution) the Government would first be appointed. The Government itself would then organize the electoral campaign for the Parliament, which would ensure the needed majority of votes. In this way grounds for fueling an improper tendency were established. Later it would be underlined even more distinctly in the formation of a too large group of voters, who voted always in favor of the ruling party or coalition.

We can count on the fingers of one hand the cases when Parliamentary elections in Bulgaria were won by the opposition. This can hardly be explained (and if so, will be a rather simple explanation) only by pre-election terror committed by the police and forged ballots. It is true that fear existed, and that it paralyzed the free will to choose. There was something else as well. After many centuries without his own state and his own politicians, it seemed that the Bulgarian citizen had acquired the habit of power and its institutions being imposed from "above" – somebody else who chose who was to rule. It seemed that he was called upon only to confirm the choice that had already been made. Even this was too much because he was in reality deprived of that right. It turned out that the right to choose still did not provoke the wish for participation; it did not mean that one could choose and would do so conscientiously. The pragmatic motive to vote in favor of those who were ruling is often found in the history of Bulgarian elections.

With the end of the Regime of the Commissions, which proved unsound and inadequate in the prevailing Bulgarian conditions at the end of 1883, the repealed regulations of parliamentarianism in political life were restored. Regardless of the fact that the old constitutional regulations were restored, the variance which arose among the Liberals during the short period of the Monarch's regime became deeper. This conflict sharpened substantially when Dragan Tzankov accepted the offer of Alexander I and formed a new Government.

The Liberals were, in practice, split into two wings. The first—ruling and small in number (also called "contented") headed by Dragan Tzankov—were ready to make certain compromises with the Monarch and the Conservatives for eventual changes in the Constitution. The second—Liberals in opposition ("discontented") – were led by P. Karavelov. To them any change in the basic Law was absolutely unthinkable and absurd. They called the Turnovo Constitution "ideal regulations, that can only make happy, enrich and make a model out of Bulgaria".[8] The Conservatives were their irreconcilable opponents in the pre-election campaign.

We can shed light upon the picture of the political dispositions in Bulgaria during the 1880's if we study the results of the Parliamentary elections for the Fourth National Assembly held in 1884.[9] The Liberals, especially the "discontented", gained a significant advantage, which was indicative of the political orientation of the majority of the electorate.

The Conservatives, having a foreboding of failure even before election day, were seeking the reason for the expected result. Quite naturally for them, it could be found in the Election Law, which "was not based on our life, on our manners and customs" and was not drawn upon from Bulgarian history. Their failure in Sofia would be explained by the fact that there Jews and Gipsies voted most actively there. The Jews—out of fear, the Gipsies—through bribery, while at the same time the Bulgarians were busy ploughing and sowing their fields. The Conservatives commented that very few deputies in the past had been elected with "Bulgarian" votes.[10]

Certain regions and centers of influence of the political forces had emerged. Very often the towns of Gorna Oryakhovitsa, Elena, Tryavna and Popovo were pointed to as "fortresses" or "nests" of the Conservatives. Wealthy people had lived in these settlements proverbially from the time of the Turkish domination; now they were small enough for the Conservative spirit and customs to rule there. In nearly all of the remaining regions the Liberals won a convincing victory substantially surpassing their political opponents. A categorical victory was won by that wing of the Liberals which was led by Karavelov and was distinguished by its more radical democratic convictions and intentions. On May 27 and June 3, 1884 the Bulgarians elected 139 Liberal and 48 Conservative deputies.

The period before the elections for the Fifth National Assembly in September, 1887 was marked with dramatic days of upsurge and despair, impetus and disturbing confusion, heavy with exultation and anxiety with the Union of the Bulgarian Principality and Eastern Roumelia in 1885, the Serbo–Bulgarian war, the abdication of Battenberg, the officers' revolts in Rousse and Silistra, the non–acceptance of Valdemar of Denmark and the crowning of Ferdinand Saxe–Coburg–Gotha.

The drama of 1885–87 is perhaps unique in Bulgarian history. In 1885 Bulgaria effected the union of the two biggest regions inhabited densely by a Bulgarian population, integrating Eastern Roumelia with the Bulgarian Principality, and defended this political achievement on the battle field. The lesson given to Europe was astonishing—the Bulgarians were able to shape their own destiny outside the desires of the Great Powers. The abdication that followed and the unsuccessful attempt with Valdemar of Denmark marked only some aspects of the deepening Russian–Bulgarian conflict. The insecurity of the Bulgarian state, which remained without a monarch, was increasing. The tension was getting stronger due to the more and more hostile distinction between the already formed Liberal wings – the Karavelov's, the Radoslavov's and the Tzankov's. With the arrival of Ferdinand still unacknowledged by the Great Powers, normalization of political life began. The Liberals gathered around Stefan Stambolov, who was a well-known figure from the time of the national liberation struggle, came to power.

The elections for the Fifth National Assembly which were held on September 27 and October 9, 1887 were an indisputable success for the Government. The "*Svoboda*" (Liberty) newspaper predicted uprisings and revolts, for which the Russian government gave substantial money to "the Tzankov's traitors", at the time of the elections. "The moment is sublime and dangerous", stated the newspaper.[11]

The bloody scenes could not be avoided. In Koutlovitza, Pleven and Gorna Oryakhovitsa peasants attacked the county police stations, but were met by the police with fire. The Government handled the situation with iron gloves: "If they rise in rebellion, they will be shot like dogs."[12] The daring of Stambolov's people faced the voters with the dilemma: Russia or independent development. Tzankov's followers and the Conservatives were considered by them to belong to one and the same party—that of "the ruble men and traitors together with our false "well-wisher".[13]

The results from the elections for the Fifth National Assembly affirmed the stand of the government and made way for the active legislative work so much needed by the Principality. Despite the police intervention and the firm hand of the rulers, the election formed a representative body, which was needed for the ruling of Stambolov and Ferdinand and for stability and success for the future of the state. The balance achieved by the Government was one in which the people were prepared to support the Monarch and his Government, that it did not wish to be a toy in the hands of Russia and that "the Bulgarians are a people free for independent life".[14]

Forming of the Party System by the End of the Nineteenth Century

In the second half of the 1880's and into the 1890's, the process of formation of the political party system in Bulgaria was taking place. The two major political trends—Liberal and Conservative—followed their natural development under the conditions of dramatic events taking place in the Kingdom. They caused them and at the same time they suffered from them.

The split in the ranks of the Liberals that began in 1883–84 continued even more painfully and inimically. Being convinced Russophiles and professing more moderate political concepts, the followers of Tzankov ("the contented") were the first Liberals to be "excluded", who only in 1899 accepted the name "Progressive–Liberal Party" (PLP). In 1886–88 a group of followers of Radoslavov was formed. They announced the name of their party—the Liberal Party (LP).

In the period 1886–90, the Stambolov's Liberals, ruling actively since August 1887, established the Stambolov's People's Liberal Party (People's LP), which supported the idea of the independent, especially from Russia, development of Bulgaria and the Monarch as a requisite for the successful development of the country. The radical views of their leader for order, economic prosperity and international recognition without the obligatory participation of the "liberator" formed not only the foundations of their party ideology but moved the mechanism of the state engine during the entire period of the so–called "regime of Stefan Stambolov" (18871894).

When the People's Liberal Party was ruling it became a center of gravity for a considerable number of the lower and medium strata of society, whose aim was to get rich quick. For that reason, in the beginning of the twentieth century the People's LP gradually became a concentration defending the interests of a part of pro–Western orientated big trade and industrial bourgeoisie. Its newspaper was "*Svoboda*" ("Liberty").

In 1896 the group of Liberals around Petko Karavelov set the foundations of another party formation under the name of the Democratic Party (DP). It now would have to lead the country in successful and difficult years. Their newspaper was "*Pryaporetz*" ("Banner").

Supported by the Monarch, but not supported sufficiently by the electorate, the Conservatives established their party, forming it into an organization in 1894, when they were in power. It was named "People's", despite the concept of elitism upon which it was based. It was headed by brilliant politician—K. Stoilov, Gr. Natchevitch, I. Geshev, etc. The Conservatives came into power after the downfall of the Government of Stambolov in 1894. They were ardent partisans of the idea for rapprochement with Russia, more stringent on suffrage (they introduced a two–year qualification for settlement). They reduced the number of the deputies (one deputy per 20,000 people instead of per 10,000), established a two–chamber Parliament and increased the prerogatives of the Monarch.

The Conservatives were men of enviable education and easy circumstances for the times, having a sense of responsibility and consistently holding their ground with respect to the institutions of the church and education. In September, 1894 the first issue of the *"Mir"* ("Peace") newspaper, which became an event of importance in the history of periodicals in Bulgaria, appeared.

In that last decade of the nineteenth century new figures emerged on the Bulgarian political scene. The Bulgarian Social–Democratic Party (BSDP) was established in 1891 under the leadership of Dimitar Blagoev. The Social–Democrats drew into their ranks workers from the uprising Bulgarian factories as well as intellectuals. At the very end of the century —in 1899—the Bulgarian Agrarian People's Union (BAPU) was established. The Agrarian movement emerged and quickly grew in the bloody conflict with governmental forces during the rule of Dr. V. Radoslavov. The political Left in Bulgaria was gradually expanding.

In 1893 was established the Interior Macedonian–Edirne Revolutionary Organization (IMERO, later IMRO) was founded. Although established outside the boundaries of the Kingdom, it would play a significant role in the political life in Bulgaria and would actively interfere in the election of deputies from the South–Western regions.

In this way, at the very end of the nineteenth and in the beginning of the twentieth century in Bulgaria seven political parties were already operating: the CP, the PLP, the LP, the People's LP, the DP, the BAPU and the BSDP—following and in some way trying to copy the modern political system in Europe. Seven parties were calling upon the Bulgarian voter in the election campaigns. They all presented themselves to the people as for the common good and for the future of Bulgaria. Often there were no principal differences among the first of the listed parties and the struggle was on personal grounds among their leaders.

"Peacefully, Quietly and Perfectly Freely"

During the period of the so–called "Stambolov's regime" the Fifth and the Sixth National Assemblies were dissolved, according to the Election Law, after expiration of their mandate. This was the time when, never mind how paradoxical it might be, in order to achieve the much wanted liberal development of the economy, Stambolov resorted to the centralization of power. The struggle for political superiority was concentrated mainly on the methods for ruling. Stambolov was strongly convinced of the rightness and expedience of the policy he was following. His uncompromising attitude was the subject of continuous attacks, especially on the eve of the elections in 1890 and 1893. Although the Prime Minister himself was warning the county governors strictly to abide by the Election Law, ways to ensure the success of the deputies supported by the Government were found.[15] The mayors were advised that they would be fined if they failed to bring the peasants to the polling stations and if they did not vote for "these persons, about whom they would be told". The county governor in Rousse even threatened that there were cannons in the city and it might become very dangerous if the vote did not go in favor of the Government.[16]

The Stambolov period gave rise to a very dangerous trend in Bulgarian politics. The violence and arbitrary arrests executed by the police and the interference of administrative staff representatives in the pre-election campaign led to a "distortion" of the election returns. Often the electorate was forced to vote, which contradicted that part of the Election Law which guaranteed non–obligatory participation. The bloody skirmishes, arrests of candidates for deputies on election day, falsified counting of the ballot–papers had one goal—only "approved" candidates, governmental partisans were to be elected, thus ensuring obedience and loyalty to the government—controlled Parliament.

The aim to ensure a victory at any cost strengthened the accumulated conviction among the electorate that the final result was predetermined and it was all the same whether the voters participated or not; those in power would get their own way. The opposition newspaper *"Narodni Prava"* ("People's Rights"), organ of the LP, stated that the electorate's indifference and inactivity could be explained and be pardoned under the circumstances, which "do not favor at all free and constitutional struggle in our country".[17]

The Sixth National Assembly prepared and enacted a Law for an amendment to the Constitution by the forthcoming Grand National Assembly. According to the new edition of Article 86, Paragraphs 1 and 2, the deputies in the National Assembly would be elected on the basis of one per 20,000 population for a five–year term. In fact, the number of deputies was reduced twice in comparison with the Election Law of 1880 which was in force at the time. The term for a deputy mandate was also prolonged.[18] Indisputably these changes limited the possibilities for establishing a real political democracy. In the existing conditions of severe censorship the newspapers' criticism against the official stand of the Government during the sessions of the Grand National Assembly was weak and ineffective.

The elections that followed in the summer of 1893 for the Seventh National Assembly justified the expectations—the smaller the number of the deputies, the better able the Government was to choose those it found suitable. Once again the energetic interference of the county governors, mayors, police and army went into action. Of course, their reason was cited as "peaceful and quiet" elections, but in favor of the "approved candidates".[19] Or as Stambolov stated in a cable to all county governors, everywhere in Bulgaria, the elections passed "peacefully, quietly and perfectly freely".[20]

The firm ruling of home affairs by Stambolov, the violation of the constitutional freedoms of the citizens in daily life and during the pre-election campaigns and the general censorship were the reasons for the United Legal Opposition (ULO) to be established in 1893. It united the efforts of the followers of Dr. Radoslavov, "unionists" (politicians from Southern Bulgaria) and Conservatives. Its leaders were V. Radoslavov, Gr. Natchowitch, K. Stoilov, D. Tontchev and G. Stranski. On March 9, 1894 the "Slovo" ("Word") newspaper published the ULO platform. The efforts of the united opposition were aimed entirely against Stambolov's regime and its policy of repression. Two months later K. Stoilov was appointed by the Monarch to form a new Government. Thus a very important seven–year period vis à vis Bulgaria and the realities of the Old Continent was completed. This was a dynamic and contradictory time, which gave birth to its heros as well as to its mistakes on the tempestuous road to modern Europe.

The Majority of the People's Party

The new Government of K. Stoilov, of course, needed parliamentary support. A date was set for new elections for the Eighth National Assembly: September 11, 1894. The PLP, being already in opposition, made a decision not to participate. On the pages of its "*Svoboda*" newspaper the party called upon all its members not to vote. The followers of Stambolov declined all responsibility "for the bad consequences for the country arising from the ruling of K. Stoilov". They considered that with their refusal to take part they would save many victims, which otherwise their adherents might eventually become in the elections because of the predicted terror.[21]

The United opposition, already in power, did not come to the elections united enough. The link between the Conservatives and the followers of Radoslavov turned out to be too feeble and insufficient, probably stable enough only until the downfall of the "dictator" Stambolov. The conflicts arose mainly with regard to correlation of the party candidates in the governmental lists. Discontented with the quotas, the followers of Dr. Radoslavov presented their own electoral lists and proclamations, but in the name of the PP or as "governmental" candidates. The final result for the Radoslavov's supporters was 37 deputies of the majority-elected governmental candidates.[22]

Fears existed regarding the influence of Stambolov's followers. Their leader himself was still actively accusing, threatening, attacking. In some constituencies the army and police were put into action. Tontchev was elected forcibly after a second ballot in Byala Slatina. The strong feelings of discontent forced him to give up his seat as a deputy and to resign from the Government.[23]

Being held in conditions of total denial and severe reaction against the just-overthrown regime, the elections of 1894 ended with the result of 154 deputy seats, with not a single adherent of Stambolov among them. Except for the 37 followers of Radoslavov, the governmental majority included another 26 Conservatives and 40 Unionists from Southern Bulgaria, whose convictions were very close to the PP and were supported by 15 followers of Tzankov. The Russophiles had a vast majority in the Parliament.[24]

The parliamentary opposition group consisted of 25 followers of Tzankov, 8 followers of Karavelov and 3 Social-Democrats. In the natural course of events, when on October 11, 1894 the Unionists declared to K. Stoilov that they would join the ruling party, a part of Tzankov's people followed them. The newly established PP took the lead in the state. For the first time the Bulgarian Conservatives formed a majority in the Parliament by parliamentary elections.

Two years later in the elections for the Ninth National Assembly 30% of the electorate took part (a little more as compared to 1894, when 26% of the electorate voted). The new elections gave even a bigger majority to the ruling party, which stabilized the situation in the country with a moderate course on the road to economic progress. As early as 1894 the Government gradually changed all key administrative and police posts.

Without any doubt this strengthened the positions of the ruling Conservatives and ensured their future success in new elections.[25]

Their success was really enviable. 150 out of 165 deputies supported the Government. The sparse opposition consisted of 1 Tzankovist, 2 Karavelovists, 3 People–Liberals and 2 Social–Democrats.[26]

The question was whether it was true that the Conservatives had earned such vast support during their two years in power. Hardly so, if we consider some facts. First, less than one–third of the electorate took part in the elections. It was quite possible that the major part of the remaining two–thirds did not sympathize and for that reason did not participate. Secondly, as already mentioned, the appointing of partisans to the important administrative positions ensured support for the Government; and third of all, the wide spread practice of arbitrariness, forgery of election results and bribery of voters also contributed to the distorted picture of the election results, as a reflection of political preferences. The results from the Parliamentary elections in 1896 gave the Conservatives a vast majority in the National Assembly and, therefore, the opportunity to govern the country undisturbed during the next three years.

CHAPTER II
1899–1914: THE NATIONAL IDEAL
AND THE CHOICE OF THE BULGARIANS

Towards More Active Participation

The rapid economic development of Bulgaria by the end of the Nineteenth century gave rise to a new European attitude—they began to speak about the "Bulgarian wonder". In the 1890's the impossible customs restrictions imposed by the Ottoman Empire were eliminated. This ensured protection of the local production from foreign competition. A special law was passed to encourage local industry—in the cities chambers of commerce were organized. The general economic advance was best seen in industry; the number of large industrial enterprises was increased five times. The credit system was modernized, the commercial turnover was enlarged. The initial symptoms of capitalism emerged.

Life, mainly in the towns, changed beyond recognition. New buildings were constructed—centers for state and social activity. The first tramways appeared in Sofia, the first cinema opened in Rousse, balls and entertainments became part of the life of "high society". Attempts to imitate Europe and the wish to modernize urban living standards often were tragically comic. But the changes both visible and hidden were obvious. In the streets, at home, in the clothes, in the conversations, in the behavior, in the thoughts. Gradually the Bulgarians were changing from observers into contemporaries of, citizens of, the European continent, choosing a proper way of development for their country.

The existing statistics for the results of the deputies' elections in Bulgaria in the period from 1899 to 1914 show the degree of activity of those who had the right to vote and the dynamics of change. A certain variation can be observed in the percentage of participation, especially on the eve and during the first years of the twentieth century when it approached 50%, then dropped a small percentage. The absence of a law to force the electorate to vote makes it possible for us to determine the attitude of the Bulgarians toward political choice.

21

The Parliamentary elections in 1901, 1902 and 1903 were characteristic with respect to participation of those living in the towns.[1] These were the only examples, as we shall see later, when the urban population was voting with greater enthusiasm than the population in the rural counties. This was not due so much to the difficulties of the peasants to exercise their right to vote—remoteness of the polling stations or their inability to leave their fields. In the beginning of the twentieth century the Bulgarian towns began to assume some features characteristic of European city life, although quite feebly expressed. The aim was to get out of the country patriarchal spirit and to modernize not only the economy, but intellectual life and political activity as well.

Prior to 1913, the percentage of participation in Parliamentary elections had been changing comparatively evenly in the towns and in the villages. In the elections for the Sixteenth National Assembly in 1913, considerably more voters took part—up 7% in the towns and by 9% in the rural districts.[2] From a historical aspect, the moment was of great importance—the elections were carried out after the Balkan and Interallied wars, on July 28th, 1913, the same year the Peace treaty of Bucharest was signed ending the Balkan wars. The attempt to realize national integration of the Bulgarian people failed. The catastrophe became reality. The population became increasingly agitated and resentful. Tension was growing. Deprived of the fulfillment of the dream for a United Bulgaria, the people were angry and impatient; their greatest wish was that justice would triumph.

Three months later, on February 23, 1914, new parliamentary elections were held in which the Bulgarians registered their most active participation since the founding of this young constitutional state. It was remarkable that while in the towns 5% more voters, compared to the last elections, cast their ballots, in the rural counties the participation exceeded 70%—14% more than in the autumn of 1913.[3] Times were hard and insecure. The Bulgarians, when there was a real threat for their future, went in large numbers to cast their votes. They wanted to take part, to express their opinions, to influence by their will the political choice.

New Government - New Elections

At all elections from 1899 till 1914, excluding those in 1908 the electoral vote gave the advantage to party formations descended from the old Liberal party. The LP, the PLP and the People's LP have ruled the country in the course of the years up to the defeat of Bulgaria in the First World War. This was not by mere chance. The electorate gave their confidence to the Liberals, for they were the political bearers of the national idea; they were relied upon to fulfil the program for the liberation of those Bulgarians who remained under foreign domination. The LP of Dr. V. Radoslavov, the PLP of Dr. Tzankov and the People's LP of Dimitar Petkov all exemplified the aspirations of the different strata of Bulgarian society for realization of the ideals from the Bulgarian Renaissance of placing Misia, Thrace and Macedonia in the boundaries found on the map from San Stefano.

At the electoral competitions in 1899 the Liberals—followers of Radoslavov—were the undisputed winners. Notorious as among the "most violent", the elections for the Tenth National Assembly were preceded by intense agitation on behalf of the LP, the ruling party at that time. Promises for firm obedience to the Constitution, appointment of honest and experienced persons to responsible positions, a guarantee of civil rights and friendly relations with the governments of every country were laid down in the pre–election program of the LP candidates in Sofia.[4]

The Liberals won the majority of the seats in the Tenth National Assembly, ensuring parliamentary support for the Government. The choice, according to the government paper, represented "a referendum, in favor of the Ministry of Mr. Grekov and Mr.Radoslavov".[5] The People's LP was the second largest Parliamentary power.

The People's Party, which had been ruling until recently, was pushed out of the highest positions in the state (it received only ten places); the newly established Democratic Party won four.[6] Thus the Liberals— followers of Radoslavov were those who would dictate and rule (and benefit from) the state.

But this Government was also soon discredited because of its policy of taxation and the violence permitted in dealing with the peasants' discontent. The official Government of General Ratcho Petrov was appointed with its only task being to prepare and carry out the new elections on January 28th, 1901. Conditions on the day of the election were comparatively calm; arbitrary police actions were held to a minimum. The opposition gave good marks to the situation as a whole.[7] As a result, the government supporters did not win the majority in the Parliament. As a matter of fact, no single party held had the requisite number of seats; the Parliament was too "variegated" in its structure. The new Government, headed by Petko Karavelov was supported by the deputies of the DP and the newly established PLP, which represented about 40% of the parliamentary vote. The People's LP was supported by more adherents compared to 1899, and sent 24 deputies to the National Assembly. A substantial success was achieved by the Conservatives with 18.7% of the vote and 29 seats.[8]

The three newest parties in Bulgarian political life presented themselves remarkably well. Established in 1896, the DP improved its position in comparison with the last elections, winning seven times more seats and becoming co-rulers with its leader P. Karavelov as head of the Government. Even bigger was the success of the two parties that took part in elections for the first time. The PLP, which was only two years old but had well-known party leaders and traditions from the Liberal past, attained the best results and won the most mandates. BAPU, which also was just two years old but led by far less well-known politicians of insufficient political experience, manifested its intentions for stable and influential presence on the political scene. The experience demonstrated that in the beginning of the XX century the Bulgarians were ready to give their support to newly established parties and to nominate representatives among their ranks. This fact to a great extent destroyed the myth for the conservative behavior of the Bulgarian voters and their political apathy.

On the other side, the success of the newly established parties proved the need for their presence in the life of the country. Backing them were those from the social strata whose interests they would defend in future. While the PLP had been supported by a considerable part of the Liberals' electorate in the past, the BAPU emerged as a real necessity in rural Bulgaria. The Union of course relied on the numerous peasantry, which responded strongly to the rule of Radoslavov.

One year later, at the elections for the 12th National Assembly in 1902, the Progressive Liberals won many more votes and seats as a result of the fact that they were the ruling power. The Government had been headed by their party leader St. Danev since December 21, 1901. Almost 160,000 more voters cast their votes for them.[9] These were not the only votes lost by the Democrats and the People's Liberals. In 1902, 200,000 more people voted than in 1901 and it was obvious that most of them decided to give their support to the PLP. A much better result was obtained by the Conservative Party, which constituted the second largest Parliamentary group in the National Assembly. Nearly 500,000 Bulgarians voted for the right-wing Russophile political parties in the electoral competition for the

Twelfth National Assembly. The Agrarians retained their 12 seats from the previous Parliament. The Social-Democrats presented themselves better and this time won eight seats.

Again With the Ballot-Paper of Stambolov

In 1902, for the first time, the electorate in the towns exceeded 50% in participation (50.44%). Increased interest in the parliamentary elections in the towns was repeated again in 1903, when on October 19th deputies for the next Thirteenth National Assembly were elected. The conditions under which the elections were carried out were completely different from those of 1901 and 1902. After the failure of the move of Ferdinand for "patriotic concentration", on May 5, 1903 the Government was again headed by General Ratcho Petrov, but at that time the People's Liberals dominated in the new cabinet.

The position of the People's LP on the national question helped to increase the number of its adherents in the border regions—for example, in Kyustendil, Bourgas, Haskovo. In those regions middle class peasants, craftsmen, teachers, even some workers and many refugees voted for the PLP. In typically rural counties like Silistra, Kula, Lovetch etc., the peasant membership in the party increased by 25-30%. This was the reason for the increase of the number—from 18 to 22.2%—of People's Liberal deputies from the rural regions.[10]

In 1903 the Party of Stambolov marked its biggest success in parliamentary elections. With some bitterness the opposition newspaper "*Pryaporetz*" noted in its issue of October 12th, 1903: "The victory in the elections surprised the winners, that's how great its scale is". The People's LP won 132 out of 189 seats and in this way made sure of being dominant in the National Assembly in the forthcoming long period of its rule. With this reliable majority, the party governed the country for five years. This was one of the few examples in the Bulgarian political reality before the wars when the Parliament served its full term. The party, having won the support of the people, formed several cabinets during that period.[11]

Of great importance for the election result was the fact that the elections for the 13th National Assembly were carried out immediately after the outbreak of the uprising on St. Elijah's Day and Transfiguration. Again, this time at the price of human life, the question of the future of those who remained under Turkish domination—Christian fellow-countrymen—was brought to the forefront. It was logical, after the drama of the uprising—the deaths, the hopes and the columns of refugees at Bulgarian borders—to look for hope and to give the advantage to the political force that declared its determination to search for a resolution of the pressing issue. Even the name of the first leader of the People's LP stirred vivid memories of the national liberation struggles and of the faces of his perished companions. Society at that moment felt an urgent need for the strong figure of Stambolov, the revolutionary, because the liberation of the enslaved Bulgarian territories seemed so near and so possible. It was natural associations with the April Uprising of 1876 to be generated. At that time the dreams seemed even more real—the Bulgarians still living in the Ottoman Empire would have the support of the Bulgarian Kingdom, its Government, its National Assembly and its people.

The remaining Liberal parties suffered defeat. The ruling party—the PLP—received only 6 seats, the LP—9, the Independent Liberals—3, the D. Tontchev Liberals—3.[12] It was clear that the People's LP had the strongest influence among all Liberal formations. Only one year before, in the elections for the Twelfth National Assembly, the situation was just the opposite, in favor of the PLP, which had won 82 seats against 9 for the People's LP. Indisputably, it was that here the mechanism for voting acted in favor of those who held the keys of the administration and carried out the elections. It is necessary to keep in mind the practice of terror and the violations of the Election Law. Nevertheless, in the absence of the obligation to vote, it can be assumed that the electoral vote reflected the main trends of the political situation.

Just before the elections in Sofia the leaders of three parties—the CP, the DP and the PLP—made an attempt to reach an agreement for unity of action on the day of voting. In spite of the common lists, almost everywhere the united opposition acted without co-ordination and in some places even with hostility due to local circumstances such as those in Lom, Peshtera, Khaskovo, Kyustendil, Pirdop. In Sofia and Varna the opposition lost. In Svishtov and Lom the Conservatives voted for the government, and in Khaskovo and Pirdop the followers of Tzankov were "disloyal". The united opposition won in Sliven, Yambol, Kazanlak and to a certain extent in Teteven, Belogradtchik and Berkovitza. In Novoseltzi the Democrats competed mainly with the Conservatives. A sad conclusion was reached: "The united opposition was a shadow, not a reality."[13]

For the DP the results were once more the same: 7 seats (8 in 1902); the Conservative Party repeated its achievement of 1901. It was obvious that these two political powers were receiving support from the hard–core main body of their electorate; a change in preference was evident among the followers of the liberal parties and the BAPU.

Though constituted in non–parliamentary fashion and often qualified as a product of the "personal regime" of the Monarch, the Government of General Ratcho Petrov succeeded in ensuring remarkable support by the National Assembly. This did not happen in the case of the DP and the CP which maintained their loyal adherents. The liberal partisans supported, in the majority, either the LP (in 1899), or the PLP (in 1901 and 1902), or the People's LP (in 1903).

The transfer of power was accompanied by considerable large–scale job–hunting and self–seeking and by penetration of the bureaucratic stratum (mayors, deputy–mayors, officers, tax–collectors) in the ranks of the liberal parties by the end of the nineteenth—beginning of the twentieth century. Those were the perpetual supporters of the ruling parties, regardless of their ideas or the color of their banner. With no hesitation at all they changed the party preferences and slogans behind which they stood each year.

This was the reason that for a short period of time (1899–1903) the leading parties lost tens of thousands votes in the parliamentary elections. The important thing was the kind of government appointed by the Monarch, often after dishonorable ploys and complicated intrigues among the party leaders. Ferdinand's goal from the beginning was to be truly a ruling Monarch, a key man in the political life of the country. By appointing governments the Monarch indirectly dictated the results of the elections, providing the executive authority the opportunity to "elect" the legislature.

The Triumph of the Democratic Party

The destiny of the ruling People's LP was quite dramatic in the years that followed. In January, 1907 an opposition group of parties was organized. They united against the followers of Stambolov under the name "Patriotic Block". The participants were the CP, the PLP, the DP and the BWSDP (right–wing socialists or r.w.s)—party formations from the far Right to the far Left. Among them one could see the outline of a liberal party, which already was no longer hiding its sympathies for the CP. The opposition against the People's Liberals was strengthening its position every day. The tension was increasing; terrorist acts were perpetrated—on February 26, 1907 the leader of the People's LP and Prime Minister D. Petkov was assassinated. May 25, 1908 was designated as election day for the 14th National Assembly.

The results of the election were a success for the opposition parties and most of all—a striking triumph for the Democrats. Twelve years after its establishment the DP became political power number one in the country, winning almost 82% of the seats.[14] The Democrats' upsurge was irresistible. The Party paper *"Pryaporetz"* reported the event with delight. The victory was ascribed to the mass approval and confidence in the Democrats ruling the country at the time.

Analyzing the number of the candidates we can clearly outline the tactics of taking advantage of its position as the ruling party. The Democrats nominated candidates for all seats; only in very few constituencies was doubling of DP candidates admitted and because of this—splitting of votes (209 candidates for 203 seats).[15] The success of the DP was clearest in the counties of Kyustendil and Vidin, where all the seats were won by Democrats. Relatively weaker was the showing of the ruling party in the region of Shoumen, where it won less than half the seats.

The fall of the People's LP, although it looked for co-operation with some opposition powers in the pre-election struggle, was complete. Despite these attempts, discontinued after the death of its leader and, more importantly, after being out of power, the Party of Stambolov won only one seat. It held a comparatively better position only in the region of Kyustendil, where it was traditionally powerful.[16]

Failure came to the other liberal parties as well—the LP received 4.6% of the votes and sent 5 men to the National Assembly. It was most popular in the regions of Shoumen, Sofia and Bourgas, but won the least number of votes in the region of Vratza. The other liberal party, the PLP, also had to swallow the hard pill of the disappointment. Its candidates got 6.1% of the votes and 3 seats. In Vratza and Stara Zagora they fared better, but in the region of Vidin they could not score. It became obvious that these parties were forced to temporarily retire from the summit of the state authority.

The CP also lost a considerable number of its supporters, some 90,000 in comparison with 1902. This loss was even more considerable if expressed by the number of places won: a mere 7 (32 in 1902 and 25 in 1903). The influence of the Conservatives was strongest in the regions of

Sofia, Stara Zagora and Rousse. These were regions where the large commercial firms flourished where representatives of big business and landowners resided. The population there was more educated (the regions of Stara Zagora and Sofia); many groups in the area were Russophiles and conservative in their views. The inverse ratio of these prerequisites explained almost entirely the weak showing of the Conservatives in the regions of Vratza and Pleven.

In May, 1908 the BAPU emerged as the second most powerful political power. Winning the confidence of 168,186 voters (14.6%), the Agrarians took 19 seats in the National Assembly for the first time in their short nine years of existence as a political formation. The counties of Varna and Shumen were the regions that brought the greatest success to the Agrarian Party (the DP had its lowest results there). These were the vast rural regions of Ludogorie and Dobruja. The Union got its weakest support in the counties of Vidin and Vratza, where the RDP and the PLP came in second after the DP.[17]

The Radical–Democrats suffered a real fiasco with their debut. In six counties of the country they did not put forward candidates at all and therefore won no votes. But even in the places where they took part, the results were a failure—4% and not a single seat. Only in the region of Vidin did the RDP win more than 19% of the vote; for ten possible places the party set forward ten candidates. The election debut demonstrated little popularity; the best result was obtained in the birth place of Naitcho Tzanov, leader of the Party.[18]

Feeble were the outcomes for the right and left wing Socialists. They had put forward candidates for approximately one forth of the seats and won respectively 1.3 and 0.3% of the votes. In the regions of Vidin and Rousse they had no candidatures at all. The right–wing Socialists obtained comparatively better results in the region of Stara Zagora and the left–wing Socialists in the region of Bourgas.[19] The lack of mass support by the voters was due to the splitting of both Socialist wings at their Tenth congress in Rousse. Their success in 1902 (8 mandates) could not be repeated in the Parliamentary elections of 1903, nor of those in 1908.

From Majoritarian to Proportional Voting System

Reasons of a foreign political nature imposed the change of the DP Government, headed by Al. Malinov. For the success of the planned forthcoming solution of the problem for national unity, according to Ferdinand, a favorable position on the part of Russia was needed. The time of the Russophile–oriented political powers on the Right had come again. The guarantee that the Conservatives would facilitate entering of the amendments in the Constitution in favor of the Monarch was hidden behind the screen of a foreign political consideration. On March 16th, 1911 Ivan Geshov, one of the eminent CP leaders, became Prime Minister of Bulgaria. In the summer of that same year, elections for the Grand National Assembly to accept changes in the Constitution were carried out. Elections for the Fifteenth National Assembly now had to be held.

At the elections of the National Assembly in September, 1911, in two counties of the country—Turnovo and Plovdiv—the proportional voting system was tested to check its efficiency. The idea to change the then existing majority system was not a new one. It was first suggested at the end of the nineteenth century by the Social–Democrats and some followers of Tzankov. In the first years of the twentieth century most of the parties had publicly expressed a wish for its implementation as a means for increasing the democratic principle in the parliamentary elections. Along with the positive expectations, there were also fears which postponed its implementation in some other countries. It was tested for the first time in Bulgaria, in 1909, in some counties in the elections for municipal and district councilors. Barely into 1912, the DP Government and the PLP reformed the Legislative electoral system and in the Election Law the principle of proportional representation was laid down. It regulated the official participation of the parties in the election campaigns. Each party had to choose a color for its ballot paper and to register it in court.

The results from the elections for the composition of the Fifteenth National Assembly demonstrated the indisputable superiority of the coalition between the CP and the PLP. Together they won 52.3% of the votes and 157 seats out of 185. Once again the rule that the elections are won by the one who held them dominated. Now the expectations for a better future in Bulgaria, and most of all, for national unity, were focussed on the Russo–phile parties of the Right. Bulgarian society, consciously or by constraint, gave its support to the conservative Right.

Considerably more popular in the rural counties were the Conservatives and the Progressive–Liberals; their results in towns were far worse by 10%. In the region of Rousse the candidates of this pre–election union, competing under the majority system won a substantial victory—66% of all votes. Their support in the region of Kyustendil was weaker—43.2% of the votes. The Liberals there had maintained their strong influence among large circles of the electorate.

The opposition newspapers abounded with news about the elections. *"Den"* (Day) wrote: "The Government won, it overwhelmed all: Democrats, Agrarians, Radicals, Socialists, all." According to an issue of the DP, the most violence used toward the electorate occurred those regions where the proportional voting system was tried—in the regions of Plovdiv and Turnovo. There a victory of the opposition was expected. There were numerous scandals in those regions where the Agrarians had strengthened their position. There had been assassinations in the regions of Vratza, Pirdop, Pleven. In Rousse there were fights between Socialists and Conservatives which ended with bloodshed and arrests.[20]

In the regions of Plovdiv and Turnovo the results for the CP and the PLP were lower by about 6% than the average for the country. It was evident that those set forward as candidates of the Union were winning with their authority rather than with the party ballot–papers with the CP label. Although it was a ruling party, the CP did not put forward candidates for all seats, 177 of the 185 possible. Only 20 of them failed to win a deputy seat. Furthermore, for those who lost an average of 8.876 votes were given, more than for those who had been elected (average of 4.277). This dramatic difference could be due to one reason only: mistakes in the pre–election tactics of the party headquarters which did not consider the specific conditions in some of the counties.[21]

The Democrats, the Liberals and the Radical–Democrats who remained in opposition were separated in the pre–election campaign; often they fought among themselves to the advantage of the ruling parties. Their defeat, according to the Democrats, was due mainly to theories, modern at that time, "for independent work in the elections, for throwing away the compromises". Socialists, Radicals and Agrarians adopted special decisions in favor of those theories. The followers of Radoslavov and Stambolov were given instructions to fight especially against the Democrats.[22]

The three liberal parties presented themselves very poorly. The results demonstrated that they had comparatively more supporters in the towns. The followers of Radoslavov were most popular in the region of Plovdiv; the followers of Stambolov and the Young Liberals in the region of Kyustendil. The Conservative party which had ruled until recently had to put up with only 4 seats in the Parliament, giving way even to the LP and the People's LP. Similar to the Liberals, the Democrats received support from the towns and that was quite natural—the interests of those who lived in the cities were defended by the DP.

The Agrarian Union again exceeded by 14% the votes cast, but in contrast to 1908, won only four agrarian deputies. In a sense the failure of the Agrarians was unexpected by the bourgeois opposition powers. In some places where, in the elections for the Fifth Grand National Assembly in the summer of the same year, the candidates of the BAPU won thousands of votes, now they had hardly one or two hundred votes. From 50 places in the Grand National Assembly the Union had lost too much, they were reduced to 4 seats in the Fifteenth National Assembly. The only explanation for this could be the violence and forgery engaged in on behalf of the Government.[23] The strong support for the BAPU was preserved in the Northeastern regions—Rousse, Shoumen and Varna.

The Radical–Democrats once again remained with no representative in the Parliament. The county of Vidin supported them most heavily, but in Shoumen they did not win a single vote.

The left–wing parties on the political scene suffered another failure. Right and left wing Socialists would not have representation in the Parliament. Receiving respectively 2.5 and 2.6% of the votes, they continued their ideological arguments and were unable to extend their influence. Considerably more voters supported them in the towns where large groups of workers in plants and factories organized trade unions. The right–wing Socialists did best in Vratza and Stara Zagora, and the left–wing Socialists in Bourgas.

The Parliamentary elections in 1911 sanctioned the change of the Government, instituted by the Monarch. One more of the goals was achieved—a possible support of Russia in the forthcoming military operations in the Balkans. All political parties expressing sympathies with the West were pushed back, away from the center of power, their participation in the governmental bodies insignificant. Ruling until recently, they suddenly lost tens of thousands of adherents, partly due to their having been discredited as rulers, partly because they had already lost the power. Only the Agrarian Party maintained its constant number of supporters and its position as the second political power in agrarian Bulgaria. After the final splitting of the BSDP in 1903, now for the second time a Social–Democrat would not cross the threshold of the National Assembly as a deputy. On the eve of decisive events for the country, political parties from the Right, led by King Ferdinand, stood at the helm of power.

The Guilty Must Lose

The Balkan wars from 1912–1913 struck the fatal blows which destroyed the Ottoman Empire and reshaped the borders on the peninsula. The consequences of these wars affected to great extent the future development of the Balkans and exerted a strong influence on Bulgarian society. Hardly convinced of the historical justice of the liberation of their fellow–countrymen in Macedonia from centuries–old Turkish oppression, the Bulgarians were too quickly placed in a desperate situation vis à vis their neighbors. The great fighting spirit, the acts of bravery which astonished the world, the delight and exultation of the liberated, turned out to be insufficient.

In 1912 Bulgaria was economically the best of the developing Balkan states, with an advanced infrastructure, solid governmental structure, finances and an already normally functioning mechanism of parliamentary political life. Directed toward its future rapid development, Bulgaria strongly believed that the time to unite the Bulgarians who remained outside its borders had come at last.

The events that followed in the summer of 1913 were dazzling. The Government was changed even before the signing of the Bucharest peace treaty. Once again a government was appointed which did not have a majority in the National Assembly, but was burdened with the difficult problem of signing the treaty. The new Prime–Minister, Dr. Radoslavov, and his Liberal Government assumed power with no illusions. The guilt for the failure was laid upon Conservatives and Progressives. They would carry the blame for diplomatic stupidities, for inconsistent military decisions, for the disorganization of the army and the country as a whole. Now the Bulgarian people would be summoned to give their support to the "spotless" Liberals.

The elections for the 16th National Assembly were held on November 24th, 1913, in conditions of deep despondency and increasing feelings of guilt in both social and political life. This syndrome, the need to accuse and punish the guilty, and the belief that this would purify and calm the Bulgarian spirit, would prevail in this land for years to come. Panic-stricken by the unexpected turn of events, feeling dissatisfied and disap–

pointed, the Bulgarian electorate went to the ballot–boxes. The participation of the voters immediately jumped by eight points. This was felt most strongly in the regions of Stara Zagora and Shumen, where the percentage of those that voted exceeded 60%.[24] Considerably more active were the voters from the rural areas—an increase of almost 10% (as in 1911) among the peasant population.

Only two years after the last Parliamentary elections and the brilliant election victory, the CP and the PLP suffered total defeat. There can be no better illustration than the figures. While in 1911 both parties in coalition won more than half of the votes of the participating electorate, they now participated separately and their results were respectively 4.5% for the CP and 2.2% for the PLP.[25] The similar decrease in supporters (–227 545) was very symptomatic and indicative. Compromised, the former rulers were forced to retire, although temporarily, from the center of the political scene.

The Liberal parties (LP, People's LP and PLP) decided to unite their efforts to win a majority in the Parliament to support V. Radoslavov. The coalition won only a little more than one third of the votes (38.2%), which made the position of the Government quite unstable. As before, the Liberals got their most powerful support in Kyustendil (48.4%) and in Shumen (46.0%) as well as in the cities as a whole.[26] Their success in the region of Turnovo was weaker due to the great popularity of the Social–Democrats there and in the region of Vidin, where they met strong resistance from Radical–Democrats. The relative election superiority of the Liberal coalition was due to the final result of the Interallied War and the failure of the politics of the Russophile parties, and their continued popularity in Bulgarian society. A hope was reborn that in a ruling position the Liberals would repeat their earlier achievements.

We can assume that in 1911 those who voted for the three liberal parties were their most zealous adherents and they had supported them again in the new elections. In November, 1913, the right to vote was exercised by almost 39,000 more voters. Even if they had all supported the liberal coalition, there was still an impressive group of about 90,700 who always preferred the ruling party. Probably this figure was a bit higher, having in mind that all other parties had considerably improved their results in comparison with 1911—the left and the right wing Socialists increased the number of their voters by several times. Considerable improvements were achieved by the Agrarians, Democrats and Radical–Democrats. In spite of everything some new voters had supported the Liberals too.

As was mentioned earlier, in the 1913 elections the DP demonstrated that it was in a process of restoration and had improved its position in society. Naturally it was looking for greater popularity in the towns, where most of its members worked. Its electoral successes were in Sofia and Kyustendil.

With its 20.9% the BAPU remained firmly on second place. The Agrarians, supported mainly by the numerous peasantry, moved seriously toward active participation in the political life of the country. In the villages more than 25% of the electors frankly demonstrated their sympathies for the Agrarian Union, the natural interpreter of their interests. The results from the elections showed that the main political powers, competing among themselves for influence in the rural counties, were the Liberals and the Agrarians.

It was not like that in the towns. There the most serious pre-election opponents of the liberal coalition turned out to be left and right wing Socialists. It was there that the working class was concentrated; at the same time most active in the pre-election campaigns were the workers organized into trade unions, compared to those who were dispersed in small work-shops and shops without a trade-union commitment. The right-wing Socialists again registered their strongest influence in the regions of Vratza, Turnovo and Stara Zagora. These counties formed their traditional regions of influence. The left-wing Socialists, as in 1911, reached their peak in the regions of Bourgas and Pleven.

What was the reason for the great "burst" in the electoral result for right and left wing Socialists? For two years their adherents increased in number more than four times nationally and substantially more in the villages. The indisputable reason for their increased popularity was the anti-war propaganda which found rich soil among the ordinary people. It was one thing to raise slogans against the war when such action served the long cherished dream for national unification—at that time the losses were left somehow in the background. The victims and the devastation were much heavier and more unbearable and more and more of those who had suffered the most now listened to the anti-war propaganda; the losses had become a reality.

On the Eve of the War

Three months later the tendencies in electoral behavior exhibited found their most categorical confirmation. It was natural for the Liberal Government of V. Radoslavov to look for more stable parliamentary support to carry out its policy. All the more so now that the rumble of the forthcoming world conflict could be heard. For the first time in the electoral history of Bulgaria, at the parliamentary elections for the Seventeenth National Assembly on February 23rd, 1914, more than 67% of the voters went to the ballot boxes.[27] Such an unprecedented throng of voters was evidence of the feeling for the forthcoming hardships and the established electoral process. The election was not something distinct and abstract, for which one had to abandon his job for a whole day. Now the Bulgarian as a real citizen of a parliamentary state went to the polling station with a clear feeling for participation in politics and for the importance of this event in his life.

In their first participation in elections in the Bulgarian Kingdom, the new counties of Gyumyurdjina and Struma, the only ones that were included in the country after the wars of 1912–1913, marked the highest degree of voter participation. More than 80% of the electorate in these regions voted for the Bulgarian National Assembly. From "the old" counties, once again, the most active was the county of Stara Zagora, although increased interest was registered in every county. In the three months following the last elections for the 16th National Assembly, the right to vote was given to an additional 19,300 Bulgarian men, and in February 1914 in "the old" counties voters who went to the polls increased by 105,700.[28]

In fact, if we compare the results with those from 1913, we can easily see that the sharp change was due mainly to the rural counties rather than to the towns. While the towns had increased their participation by 5%, in the villages the activity of the voters had increased by more than 14%.

Both in the rural and in urban polling stations, all political parties, excluding the Socialists, had received more votes. This time the latter were losing the battle not only by per cent of the vote, but also by the number of votes. Preserving their traditional superiority in the corresponding counties, they demonstrated a lower degree of popularity and in the new counties, in practice, they had no support at all. In the beginning of 1914 the appeals against the war had weakened. The slogan for a Balkan federation turned out to be out of date at a time when Europe was rapidly heading toward a war and the alteration of state borders. The refusal to trust the left–wing parties demonstrated something else, as well. Bulgarian society, at this historical moment, although still bearing its grief from 1913 was again hoping for national unification with its fellow–countrymen who had remained beyond the borders of the Fatherland. This society imposed its revived hopes on the Liberal Government and the other right–wing parties.

The liberal coalition had marked a better result. As could be expected, the new counties, especially Gyumyurdjina, supported the ruling party most strongly. It was obvious that the other parties were not well known there and thus had no adherents. The opposition aimed its angry attacks against the followers of Radoslavov, blaming them for the manipula–tion of the Turkish–speaking population in the new regions. In the papers an Appeal was published, a translation from Turkish, written by the Turkish notables in Gyumyurdjina. In Gyumyurdjina, rich men and beys gathered together and placed on the ballot list the names of 12 Moslem men for deputies and decided to collaborate with the present Government. How to vote was explained; threats were made. Interference by the army in the pre–election campaign in the new Bulgarian territories was mentioned.[29] Later on the success of the Liberals in these elections would often be explained and excused by the Turkish votes from Gyumyurdjina.

In this region by the Aegean Sea only the DP, out of the remaining political powers, succeeded in winning enough votes and—in Struma—even to be a worthy rival and competitor of the Government ballot. The opinion was that, in the county of Struma, the DP had won the Bulgarian vote, while the Government had won the Turkish vote, was wide spread. As a result—9 seats were won by the followers of Radoslavov and 8 from the Democrats.[30] In the remaining part of the country the Liberals reached an increase relatively the same as that in 1913. The most massive support for the ruling party was in the region of Shumen. As a comparison, the united Liberals were liked better in the towns than in the villages (49 to 44%).[31]

Ranked second again, the BAPU received its strongest support in the regions of Rousse and Shoumen and in the rural counties as a whole. Comparatively weaker was its representation in the county of Vratza. It is probable that its results would have been better if it had established organizational structures and a reputation in the newly annexed territories. The Union did not participate in the electoral contest there at all and naturally did not win any votes.

The DP ranked third according to its election success. It continued the successful course of its election results—from 5.1% in 1911, 7.9% in 1913 to 11.2% in 1914.[32] The upsurge in the political prestige of the Democrats was due partly to the failed politics of the CP and the PLP and, to a great extent, to their established and permanent presence and their loyal supporters. Statistics show that the DP could rely on the votes of the town businessmen, merchants and officers and these of those of the middle class landowners and municipal officials in the villages. Excluding the region of Struma, they presented themselves quite well, as before in the regions of Sofia and Kyustendil.

The Conservatives and Progressives continued to be ignored. The failure in 1913 was heavy as a mill stone; it compromised them and left the politicians of these two Russophile parties in unfavorable positions. Already regarded as failures, they were obviously supported only by their most zealous adherents. They were much more popular in the towns where the bankers, owners of big enterprises and prosperous merchants lived, than they were in the villages. Only in the county of Varna, both parties reached an agreement and participated in a coalition in the elections, but their success was very limited. The Conservatives in the region of Sofia and the Progressives in the region of Vratza achieved considerably good results.

The elections for the Seventeenth National Assembly, held in February, 1914 on the eve of the forthcoming world war exposed the situation of the political dispositions and preferences of the Bulgarian electorate at that moment. Once again, as many times before, advantage was given to the Liberals—this time ruling the country in coalition. The Agrarian Union persuasively won second position, relying on the stable support of the Bulgarian villages, suggesting its potential capacity to increase even more its influence in this agrarian country. The DP gradually regained its positions from the past, overcoming its loss of power and led by bright political personalities like Al. Malinov, A. Lyaptchev, N. Mushanov. The former rulers of Bulgaria—also led by prominent politicians like I. Evstatiev Geshov and Dr. St. Danev—were disregarded by the electorate that had supported them so energetically in 1911. The development of events in 1913 determined the dissatisfaction with them and pointed the people's hopes in another direction. The Socialists too were rapidly losing their adherents—for three months nearly half of their voters turned away, supporting others, or did not vote at all. The socialist propaganda was not obviously functioning.

The times had changed—hopes again were revived for a fair solution of the national problem and this did not exclude military actions.

The elections in 1914 marked a peculiar peak in the participation of the electorate. Until that moment the Bulgarian people had never voted in such large numbers. It was as if the Bulgarians sensed the dramatic nature of the months before the war and that it would be necessary for this newly elected Assembly to work longer—in the next five hard years. Because of Bulgaria's involvement in the World War in 1915 for a long period of time there would be no possibility of holding new parliamentary elections. Restless and anxious about the destiny of his state, at a disturbing time and among hostile neighbors, the Bulgarian voter once again gave his support to the Government.

CHAPTER III
1919-1934: MULTIVARIETY OF CHOICE

Restoration of the Parties after the War

The end of the First World War found Bulgaria economically destroyed, politically unstable and having gone through two unsuccessful efforts for national union. The contradictive social structure of the Bulgarian society remained and the party formations entered the next period at the start of a new situation in the country and in Europe. The regime of King Ferdinand was ended. He abdicated in favor of his elder son Boris. However, several difficult years for the throne had yet to pass before rule by monarchy would again become a political factor in Bulgaria.

The Right-oriented political parties fell into a deep crisis. Four of them—the Conservative (*Narodnyashka*) Party, the Democratic Party, the Progressive-Liberal Party and the Radical Party formed the so-called "Entente" parties' group because of their foreign orientation. They were not those who had to bear the disgrace for the fatal commitment of Bulgaria to the Triple Alliance; they upheld friendship with England and the U.S.A. In the course of two years—1918 and 1919—those parties formed three governments led by Malinov and Kostourkov and two others led by Theodor Theodorov. The single goal of those cabinets was clear—the sinking ship had to be saved. This group of parties played a much larger role in the political struggles of the country compared to the Liberal parties' group during the period 1919-1934. The first group was much stronger and represented one of the major factors in the consolidation of the political forces on the Right during the early post-war years.

The most influential among them was the Democratic Party. It restored its regional organizations more quickly and more actively in comparison with the others. Co-ruling the country, together with the Radical Party (the Malinov-Kostourkov cabinet), it participated in dealing with the Soldiers' uprising and in saving the crown. In 1920 the Democratic Party had at its disposal a network of 1,790 local organizations (covering all regions) and 62,886 members.[1] The most popular leaders of the Democratic Party were Al.Malinov, A.Lyaptchev, N.Moushanov, G.Danailov, Vl.Mollov, Dr.

41

P.Orachovatz, Al.Girginov, Gr.Vassilev. The party color was purple and the party newspaper—"*Pryaporetz*". The party color was very important for the proportional electoral system then in force. Often the political parties were identified by the color of their ballots.

Members of the Conservative Party, as before, were the representatives of the more well–to–do groups in Bulgarian society and the intelligentsia closely connected with them. There were also members of average and small resources, but this party owed its characteristics to the representatives of big business. Immediately after the war, experienced politicians like Iv.Geshov, M.Madjarov, Th.Theodorov, the Bourovs, the Vazovs and others formed its leadership. The Conservative party had a great influence on the high officers of the military reserves. Politically, the efforts of the Conservatives and most of the others were directed towards unity of the political powers on the Right in Bulgaria to strengthen the position of big business against radicalization of the poor people in the towns and villages, against the tendency of transition of political power to the Left, to the Agrarian movement, which was increasingly gathering strength and actively confirming its presence.

On December 5th, 1920 the Conservative party and another Entente party—the Progressive–Liberal Party—united under the name United Conservative–Progressive Party (UCPP) with the Conservative Party statutes and the Progressive–Liberal Party platform. They accepted the blue Party color of the Conservatives and the Party newspapers "*Mir*" and "*Bulgaria*". The new formation was a political organization of Bulgarian big business— with more important representatives than in the other parties, i.e. the banks, commercial companies, industrial and agrarian businesses in the country.

On June 21st, 1918 the Radical Party came into power for the first time, but possessing relatively small influence in the government. In a Resolution accepted by its High Party Council it was stated that because of the situation created by the war and the signing of the peace treaty, the Party's participation in the cabinet which originated from the bloc of the Entente parties was necessary and imperative.[2] From the end of 1918 until the beginning of 1919, the Radical Democratic Party succeeded in restoring its organizations in most of the villages and towns and even created new ones, including Eagen Thracia and the Edrene region. Members of this party were small traders, clerks, lawyers, teachers and average and small agrarian owners. As a whole its pre–war social structure had been preserved.

Another section of the Bulgarian political scene was occupied by four liberal parties, three of which were clearly identified with the national catastrophe, as well as with the unsuccessful efforts for a territorial solution of the Bulgarian national problem (discussed in Chapters I and II). These were the Liberal Party (LP), the People's Liberal Party (the Petkovists—PLPp), the People's Liberal Party (the Genadievists – PLPg) and the Young Liberal Party (YLP).

Having in mind that for the moment they had been rejected by the major portion of Bulgarian society, in November, 1920 they united in one political formation—the National Liberal Party (NLP). In its program the Party proclaimed itself to be in favor of changing the Neuilly Peace Treaty, for Bulgaria's membership in the Organization of Nations, for progressive reforms in government and for Constitutional guarantees for the citizens and against Bulgarian capital flowing abroad.[3] The Party color was green. P.D.Petkov, N.Genadiev, M.Hranov, St.Doichinov, D.Vurbenov, B.Smilov were elected members of the Standing Committee.

The appearance of the UCPP and NLP represented the beginning of a consolidation process among the political forces on the Right in the country, gradually recovering after the war, gathering strength for revenge against the expanding influence of the Left–oriented parties.

After the October revolution in Russia in 1917, the party of the left–wing Socialists changed its name to the Bulgarian Communist Party and energetically embarked upon a program of "Leninization". The unstable political situation, the ruined economy, the mass impoverishment after the war and the crisis in fulfillment of the national ideal of "San Stefano Bulgaria" provided suitable soil for more intensive propaganda among the people and the army. The anti–war Party slogans made more and more people realize the nonsense of the European butchery.

The Bulgarian Agrarian People's Union participated as well. Until the Soldiers' uprising (1918), the BAPU's leaders Daskalov and Stamboliiski, were in disgrace, but the wide–spreading Agrarian movement soon became the major political factor in Bulgaria. The two main principles, stated in the Union's program and approved by the leadership in 1919 were: 1. the principle of rule by the people and 2. the "labor property" principle against big business landownership and against the abolition of private property. In comparison with the Agrarian Parties in Czechoslovakia, Yugoslavia and Poland the BAPU program was substantially more democratic and the organization more progressive.[4] The natural post–war development in

Europe pushed to the forefront the more radical political forces in Bulgaria
as well. First the BAPU participated in a coalition government, then it ruled
the country independently for three years.

On to the Ballot–Boxes Again

During the First World War parliamentary elections were not
conducted in Bulgaria although the term of the National Assembly was over.
The Seventeenth National Assembly was in session; it had been elected on
the eve of the War in 1914. At the end of the war some political parties
declared themselves against holding new elections before the peace treaty
was signed, the new boundaries of the state were defined and the prisoners-
of–war returned. Those parties were the Democratic Party, the Conservative
Party and, to a certain extent, the liberal parties. They felt they were not
prepared; that they needed more time in order to realize the best results for
them.

The PLP and the RDP wanted immediate elections. The latter published
its pre–election program on August 1st, 1919 in Bulgarian and in Turkish.
In their platform the Radicals' stand was for "people's rule" and deep social
reforms to be realized in a parliamentary, constitutional way and was
categorically against the goal pursued by the Communist Party—establishment of a Soviet type of government in Bulgaria—and against the BSDP's
socialism. It favored keeping private property especially in the field of
agriculture.[5]

On the eve of the August elections of 1919, the traditional parties of the
Right published several proclamations, very often directed towards the
BAPU, the BSDP and the RDP as well as against the BCP. An appeal was
directed to all Bulgarians, no matter their class position, to unite for the sake
of saving the mother country, for a just peace and good relations with the
Entente countries, for social solidarity, strict adherence to the Law and
morality.[6]

The BSDP, then participating in government, was favored in the
pre–election campaign—it held the Ministry of the Interior with Krustyu
Pastuchov in the position of Minister. Of the 84 counties in the country
there were 52 counties in which BSDP representatives were heads of the
police, 14 counties had police superiors from the BAPU, 5 from the CP, 2
from the PLP, 6 from the RDP and 4 places were vacant.[7] That situation
would inevitably influence the election results.

The election on the 17th of August, 1919 was carried out following the proportional system which was already established in Bulgaria. In order to vote, one had to be male, over the age of 21, with civil and political rights according to the Turnovo Constitution. The party formations participated separately without any bloc or other pre–election party unions. The more radically oriented parties were in a hurry to hold the elections, having in mind the post–war mood of society. The parties on the Right, as a whole not yet organizationally restored, some of them having been discredited in the recent past, insisted the elections be postponed. Nevertheless all of them put forth their candidate lists. For the first and the last time in the history of Bulgaria, on the 17th of August 1919, the population from the Edirne district voted.

Compared to the last pre–war election in 1914 for the Seventeenth National Assembly, the number of voters in Bulgaria five years (four of them in wartime) later had increased from 1,146,880 to 1,203,745. However the percentage of participation indicating the political activity of the population had been reduced considerably—from 67.1% in 1914 to 54.5% in 1919. This may be explained by a number of reasons: hopelessness after the war and the unsuccessful effort for national unity, electoral lists that were inaccurate because of the war victims and the prisoners–of–war and last, but not least, it was a time of hard work in the fields which hampered the voter participation of the peasants. In spite of these problems the rural electoral colleges' participation was higher than that of the urban. The most active voters were in the Stara Zagora and Pleven districts and in the new Edirne district.

The election results in general showed a clearly expressed shift to the Left in the preferences of the electorate, toward the BAPU and the BCP. The Agrarian Union received an average of 26.8% of the votes in the country and the BCP, 18.2%. The anti–war propaganda, the economic destruction and the international situation of Bulgaria served to point the Bulgarian electorate towards the radical revolutionary propensities. The success of the Agrarian Party in the various parts of the country was highest in the Shumen district at 49.3% and in the Varna district at 40.3%. The greatest number of followers of the Communists was in the Bourgas and Vidin districts, 32.3% and 26.7% respectively.[8]

According to the announcements in the Agrarian Union newspaper "*Zemedelsko zname*" those results had been expected, but they could have been even better. The newspaper's comments on the BCP participation in the electoral competition are interesting because they try to explain why the Communist Party did well enough to come in second. "The great number of votes in the towns were given to the Communist Party. Almost the entire alien population in the towns had voted for them. In the town of Pleven all the Gipsies, Turks and Jews had balloted for the Communists. The Gipsies in all villages had voted for them as well; also, all former followers of Radoslavov, Tonchev and Petkov voted in favor of the Communists. In all villages where these parties had priority before, the Communists now prevail and the Liberals have not got a single vote. On the road to this success, the left–wing Socialists could not be stopped by anything. There is no other party using deception and delusion in such a reckless manner as they. In many places they convinced the Liberals that Stamboliiski had been thrown out of Paris and that Thracia, Kyustendil, Tzaribrod and Vidin had been already occupied by Greeks and Serbs etc."[9]

The Parliamentary seats were distributed among the parties as follows: 85 for the Agrarians, 47 for the Communists, 39 for the Social–Democrats, 28 for the Democrats, 19 for the Conservatives, 9 for the Radicals and 8 for the Liberal–Progressivists.

The average percentage of votes for the country polled by the Social–– Democrats was 12.8% (or 84,185 votes) which in fact meant they doubled their electoral result from 1914. Now however the situation was fundamentally different. The BSDP had much bigger expectations but its candidates polled only 29.0% in the Gyumyurdjina district. The RDP was dissatisfied as well, expecting a success of 15–20 seats.[10] The Radicals managed to expand the pre–war result of the RDP by about 1.5% – 5% (33,861 votes) for the country, having kept their traditional strong support in the Vidin district—16.3%.

The old parties from the Entente camp and their electoral results indicated that the DP and the CP were relatively the most influential among them with 10.2% (66,953 votes) and 8.8% (57,907 votes). In comparison with the pre–war elections the Conservatives had increased the number of their adherents by about 18,900, but the Democrats had lost nearly 19,650 of theirs. Nevertheless both of them—the largest Entente parties—gained the highest results in the same districts—Gyumyurdjina and Sofia.

The Parliamentary election in August, 1919 was a major failure for the "catastrophe" camp parties—the "national" parties. Having ruled the country unsuccessfully during war–time, they were now deprived of the people's confidence in them. It was the first time since their establishment that the

Liberal and the Young–Liberal Parties did not send a deputy to the National Assembly. The NLP (Genadievists) took one seat and the NLP (Petkovists) were marginally more successful with two parliamentary places.

Analyzing the results we can ascertain that (1) those votes lost by the Democrats had been diverted to the CP and the RP; (2) the Liberals' firm electorate was reduced to 39,143 votes or 5.9% and (3) those voters disappointed with the policy of the Liberals and those who usually cast their vote for the government—about 306,500 in number—had for the most part given their votes to the Agrarian candidates and partially to the Social-Democrats and the Communists, or did not vote at all.

To the Left Rather Than to the Right

On the 21st of February, 1920 the Eighteenth National Assembly was dissolved before the end of its term by a decree signed by King Boris III. The new parliamentary elections were fixed for the 28th of March, 1920.[11] The Decree dissolving the Assembly was accompanied by a report written by Prime Minister Alexander Stamboliiski. It covered the motivation and the need for new elections. It stated in part: "The present National Assembly does not correspond to the real will of the Bulgarian people, this can be accounted for from the results obtained at the municipal and district elections already being carried out. A new check–up of this will is necessary which will create a parliament really corresponding to this will and a stable government which will start in firm steps the reforms in all spheres of ruling the state."[12]

The Agrarians believed firmly that the new count of the votes would be in favor of their union and they would have at their disposal a satisfactory majority in the future National Assembly. They would need this to fulfil the tasks involved in their 1919 program. The "stable" government would be one dominated in general by the BAPU. The correction made in the Electoral Law gave them grounds for hope and belief in the complete success of the election campaign. Introducing the obligatory vote would most benefit the ruling party.

The election for the Nineteenth National Assembly was held on the 28th of March, 1920. According to the Electoral Law in force at that time, which was published in the State Gazette No.264, February 26th 1920, the right and obligation to vote was given to men over 21, excluding the police and army officers, foreign citizens, those who were convicted of crimes etc. As

the Law for change and the addition of some articles in the Electoral Law
[13] said, voting was obligatory for all who were not disenfranchised. Every
voter who did not vote without having valid reasons was fined 20 to 500
leva. It went to the municipality from which he came. Valid reasons for not
voting were: illness, death or disease of a family member, being absent too
far, insuperable obstacles and others.

Examining the circumstances under which the election was carried out
and the extent of the political activity of voters, we should have in mind the
following. In the course of those seven months between the elections for the
Eighteenth and the Nineteenth National Assemblies, Bulgaria had to sign the
peace treaty forced upon it by the Great Powers and suffered the heaviest
strike in its history—the strike of transport workers. The country was ruled
by a coalition government led by Al.Stamboliiski. With the BAPU, the CP
and the PLP took part in the cabinet. However it was obvious that the
Agrarians' influence grew bigger and bigger.

The statistical data indicate that fewer voters were registered in the
electoral lists as compared to 1919. It was a reflection of the post–war
conditions—a great number of victims, prisoners–of–war, territories torn
from Bulgaria. At the same time the electors' participation grew considerably
higher in numbers and in percentage (mostly because of the introduced
obligatory voting).

In the rural areas 215,000 voters (82.2%) cast their ballots and in the
towns 43,000 (61.1%). The political activity of the population in rural
electoral colleges was appreciably higher than the participation in the urban
colleges. On the 28th of March, 1920 the total number of voters who
exercised the right to vote was 915,172, or 77.3%. In the newly–gained
lands the percentage of participation was lower (67.5%), but the difference
between rural and urban colleges was not so considerable (68.1% and
65.4%).[14]

The electoral results showed the BAPU and the BCP as the most
significant political parties. They gained 38.2% and 20.2% respectively.
Some elements of the BAPU platform from 1919 had been included in the
coalition government program at that time. With its requirements and
aspiration towards people's rule, economic reforms, social legislation,
preservation of private property and reduction of big business the BAPU
gained more and more credit and hope for an emergence from the economic
destruction.

It should be noted that while in the rural municipalities the votes given to the Agrarian Union followed a uniform rate of growth, in the towns they showed a sharp increase having tripled nearly in comparison with 1919.

A relatively high increase in the rate of BCP adherents can be noticed in the villages, as well as in the towns. In the rural areas it was 56.5% more compared with 1919. More and more large groups of peasant small and average landowners, having voted up until that moment for the traditional Right, directed their attention and expectations towards those parties standing behind the idea of a radical change in the Bulgarians' lives.

Except in the Mastanli and Pashmakli regions (where following the "rule" the ruling party always won the victory) with 53.3% and 57.8% in favor of BAPU, the Agrarians gained convincingly in Shumen district with 56.9% and in the Varna district with 45.9% of the vote. The Communists had the greatest number of followers in the Bourgas district and in the Petrich district—29.5% and 27.7%. In the Pashmakli district they participated in the election campaign together with the Social-Democrats and were the least popular in Mastanli district (both districts were at the southern border).

The Democrats turned out to be in the best position among all political parties on the Right. As mentioned above, they had the widest well functioning organization network, stood for good relations with the Entente powers and were in opposition. Their total result for the country as a whole was 10.0%, even better than the result gained by the ruling CP and PLP. In some regions, for example in the Kyustendil district the DP obtained even more votes than the Communists.[15] The DP's candidates gained a considerable success in the Petrich and Sofia districts too—18% and 16.3% respectively. In Shoumen they formed a coalition with the CP and took 13.7% of the vote.

The Conservatives and the Progressive-Liberals, although participating in the Al.Stamboliiski cabinet, kept in general the extent of their influence from 1919 gaining 6.7% and 5.0%. The Conservatives were comparatively more influential in Sofia district and the Progressive-Liberals in Vratza. They managed to organize a coalition only in Pleven district where they had a better result than the Democrats.

The Radicals kept their position from the previous election and even improved it in some districts. The Social-Democrats, being already in opposition, suffered failure, obtaining two times fewer votes than in 1919, a return to the pre-war situation. The Radicals were pleased with the result in Vidin—15%—and the Social–Democrats in Turnovo and Vratza with 7.9% and 8.0% respectively.[16]

The liberal parties again finished last in the number of votes they received. The memory of their government and the national catastrophe that followed was still fresh; the chance for realizing the national ideal had become more distant than ever. The NLP (Genadievists) had a comparatively better result of 2.9%, while the Young–Liberals, the Liberals and the NLP–Petkovists had about 0.3% and 1.9%. The Petkovists gained 9% in Kyustendil district (the Radomir county was one out of the few in the country where the Liberals still had a considerable influence). In Rousse, Sofia and Stara Zagora districts a Liberal bloc united the Liberal adherents of all the wings and the result was a better one – 8.6%, 5.4% and 3.0%.

In the spring of 1920, for the first time, the number of those eligible who actually voted exceeded 70% and even reached the average of 77.3% for the country. The BAPU and BCP strengthened their positions as first and second most influential political forces. The convincing presentation of BAPU led to the formation of an independent Agrarian government again headed by Al.Stamboliiski. The "starry moment" of the Bulgarian Agrarian Union came – three exceptional years of independent rule were ahead, a quite remarkable event in the history of the old continent.

All the traditional Bulgarian parties on the Right appeared to be losing. Only a few of them managed to keep their results from previous elections; others continued to lose. Now, for the first time, all of them were out of power and joined the opposition. That would inevitably accelerate their efforts to consolidate organizationally and tactically, to undermine the basis of the Agrarians' regime and to restore their previous positions.

The First Referendum. White or Black?

The role of a catalyst in this process of the unification of the Bulgarian Right parties was the People's *Sgovor* founded in 1921. It was constructed as an elite organization part big business and part representatives of the intelligentsia. It was also a political formation—but not a political party—claiming to express the interests of the entire Bulgarian people.[17]

The uniting of political forces from the Right was crowned with success when on the 6th of July, 1922 the Constitutional Bloc was established. Participating in the Bloc were the Democratic Party, The United Conservative-Progressive Party and the Radical Democratic Party. The Bloc tasks were to struggle against the Agrarian government's activities and the revolutionary movement, to restore the position of big business and to take the state power in its hands. In a letter circulated by the People's *Sgovor* dated August 23rd, 1922 it was said: "The Bloc formation presents the beginning of uniting the forces of order and democracy...".

Mass actions to overthrow the BAPU government were planned. In some towns anti–government demonstrations were held. A convention of all opposition forces was set up to be held in Turnovo in September, 1922. The Agrarian government struck a blow to the Constitutional bloc with a BAPU–organized beet–producers' fair to take place at the same time and thus frustrate the Bloc's demonstration. It mobilized its "orange" Guards (the Party police) and arrested many people. The Agrarians treated the leaders of the old political parties harshly, scoffing at and mocking them. They felt powerful and tried to establish the so–called "peasant dictatorship" directed against both the Right and the Left.

Immediately after those events, in a situation of non–stop fighting against the actions of IMRO (Inner Macedonian Revolutionary Organization) bands, the first referendum in Bulgarian history was held. The people were asked to say "yes", guilty or "no", not guilty to the actions of the cabinets of Iv.Ev.Geshov, St.Danev and Al.Malinov which had led to the national catastrophe.

The Law for consulting the people about the guilt of previous cabinets' ministers was published in the State Gazette No.160 dated October 17, 1922. According to the Law, the referendum had to be held following the regulations of the municipal elections law; voting was obligatory. A white ballot was to be cast to indicate guilt and a black one to indicate not guilty. (From a psychological point of view it would have been rather difficult for voters to accept black as a symbol of innocence.) As Article 20 of this Law stated, if the referendum results for the entire country favor "guilty" then the ministers, cited in Article 1, should be tried by a special state (people's) court which would be composed by enactment of a specific law.[18]

The Constitutional Bloc denounced the Referendum, qualifying the trial as political pursuit and revenge.[19] The Social–Democrats perceived the law as non–democratic and anti–constitutional. According to the Democrats the law was a unique one, enforced by the Turnovo convention and the High Council of the BAPU. The Radicals, as well as the Liberals, rejected the law. Only the BCP supported it. The King remained quiet.

The Referendum results from November 19th, 1922 were rather indicative. On the 22nd and 24th of November the *"Zemedelsko zname"* newspaper published the following data: The total number of white ballots cast in the country was 647,313 and the black ballots—223,584. In the towns the count was white 93,632 (54.5%) and black 78,145 (45.5%); in the villages: white 554,636 (79.2%) and black 145,637 (20.8%). The government's strongest support came from the rural population which categorically rejected the state policy of 1911–1918. In the towns, however, the old political parties (the Constitutional Bloc and the National–Liberal Party) still had considerable influence. In Sofia, for example, 10,562 white ballots and 17,222 black ballots were cast. There were 2,286 ballots which were declared invalid. The Bloc also won in Plovdiv, Sliven, Kyustendil and Popovo. In Petrich and Nevrokop districts almost all votes cast were black, for the people there were dissatisfied with the BAPU's policy of normalization and improvement of relations with Yugoslavia. In Pleven, Varna, Shoumen, Rousse and Vratza districts there were not more than 150–200 black ballots cast.

On the 19th of November, the Bulgarians opposed vigorously the old policy; they favored trying those who were guilty for the national catastrophe and the post–war reparations that followed. They supported the Agrarian government. The Bloc suffered a political defeat. This was the second blow struck by the BAPU after the Turnovo events of September, 1922.

The Great Victory of BAPU

In February, 1923 the idea of dissolving the Nineteenth National Assembly before the set term finally became dominant in government circles. The most significant reason for this was the weakening of the Agrarian parliamentary group. After the changes in the cabinet made in the beginning of 1923, the new government needed strong parliamentary support to further its reform activities. In addition, the project for changes in the Constitution, on which Stamboliiski himself was working very hard, could be passed only by a large Agrarian majority in the Assembly. The time for new elections was chosen carefully, after the changes in the government had been made, the arrangement of the terms for paying reparations and the Nish agreement.

An important part of the pre–election preparation was the Law for Change and Additions to the Electoral Law passed on the 23rd of February by the Nineteenth National Assembly.[20] According to the changes not the districts, as it was then, but the administrative counties became electoral colleges. The towns of Sofia, Plovdiv, Varna and Rousse formed independent electoral counties. The entire opposition—the Constitutional Bloc, the National-Liberal Party and the Bulgarian Communist Party—opposed the Law because its purpose was clear enough. It served to profit the party which gained the majority of votes by the shifting of the electoral colleges to the counties.

On the 27th of February the opposition made a final effort to avert the elections. A delegation formed by Bloc leaders (Girginov, Moutaphov and Naidenov) was accepted by the King. They requested that the National Assembly not be dissolved and that the Agrarian government be replaced by an all-party cabinet which would conduct free parliamentary elections to calm the country. The King's reaction was one of indifference and the Nineteenth National Assembly was dissolved on the 12th of March, 1923 before the end of its term. The date for new elections was fixed by a Decree signed by Boris III—it was April 22nd, 1923.

The BAPU threw itself into the pre-election struggle. Stamboliiski, all the ministers and the members of the Standing Committee attended meetings where their speeches were enthusiastically received. The opposition press reported on disorders and illegal activities of the "orange" Guards, about "pre-election Bacchanalia, when any measure, any responsibility and any thought about the common people's and state interests had been lost".[21] Announcements about arrests of opposition candidates, including Communists, internees and the distribution of false ballots appeared. Dr. Genadiev (leader of NLP) was arrested while campaigning in Kritchim; the Bloc candidates in Rousse were interned; in Gorna Oryahovitza all public meetings were forbidden.

The poster "war" in Sofia reached its climax two or three days before the election. The trams were again decorated with orange posters. The Agrarians even published and spread an appeal signed "From a group of Bloc followers". On an orange piece of paper another short appeal was published "from a group of free-thinking Communists". Separatists-Agrarians (Tourlakov's group) published a newspaper "*Obnova*" ("Renovation") in two colors—orange and purple, the color of their election ballot.

The Communists did heavy poster propaganda, mostly in the surrounding quarters. The Social-Democrats published appeals and small posters with Pastuchov's and Sakasov's portraits, as well as an appeal addressed to the refugees and the emigrants. The Bloc's appeals were numerous, too, urging the citizens to vote the purple ballot. One of them read: "Today the Constitutional Bloc parties are carrying the cross of martyrdom because they are fighting for preserving the people's freedoms and interests."[22]

The elections were held on the 22nd of April in a comparatively normal atmosphere. The opposition press confirmed this. On that day 1,058,476 voters participated; 86.5% of all eligible voters registered in the electoral lists of the Kingdom. As compared to the previous elections in 1920, when voting was also obligatory, there was a 9.2% increase in the number who cast their ballots. It is impressive that the activity of urban voters had increased sharply—by 16%. There was a 7% increase in the rural areas. But the difference sill existed and in the villages people voted more actively than in the towns (77.5% to 89,2%). The most active urban population was that in Stara Zagora—85.3%   and the most active rural in the Vratza district—93.5%.[23]

The government's expectations were exceeded. This was also recognized by the Minister of the Interior, Christo Stoyanov, in an interview given to the "Utro" newspaper.[24] Instead of the expected 180–200 seats the Agrarians gained 212. "The victory is tremendous"; the Minister said. The Electoral Law change made on the eve of the elections produced the expected results. The BAPU obtained the necessary votes—for the first time since its establishment it gained over 50% of the vote (53.7), giving them a considerably greater parliamentary majority. Of the 245 places in the Parliament, 212 (86.5%) would be "orange". The votes of 2,684 electors stood behind each Agrarian deputy.

The Communist Party confirmed its positions from the last elections. The votes of 203,972 electors were cast in their favor (19,356 more than in 1920) with a very slight reduction in the percentage—from 20.2% to 19.2%. The Communists' showing was strongest in the Vidin and Bourgas districts and weakest in the new Mastanli and Pashmakli districts (1.7% and 2.7% respectively) and in the Rousse district (10%). The Communist parliamentary group consisted of 16 deputies, each of them elected by 12,748 voters. Due to the articles of the Electoral Law, it was a nearly five times lower electoral divisor in comparison with the Agrarian seats.

The results indicated a decrease in the Social–Democrats' influence. BSDP obtained an average of 2.6% for the country. In some regions the Socialists managed to participate in a coalition with the Constitutional Bloc and gained 3% of the votes and three places in the Parliament. Their success was especially important in the Vratza district where Pastuhov, their leader, held first position on the electoral list. The other two seats were gained in the Varna district.

It was the first time the Constitutional Bloc participated in parliamentary elections as a political formation. After the failure at the Referendum in November, 1922, the Bloc parties opposed dissolving the National Assembly before the term set and, especially, the last changes of the Electoral Law. The coalition of the political Right was supported by 166,909 voters in the country, or by 15.7%. It should be mentioned here that in those six districts where an agreement was obtained for pre-election union with the Social-Democrats, separate lists of the BSDP and the Constitutional Bloc had been registered. It is obvious that the road to a pre-election coalition had been rather difficult and that where there was no coalition agreement, the votes were split.

In the Petrich district where the BAPU was not popular because of its foreign policy, particularly after the December events in Kyustendil, the Central Committee of the Inner Macedonian Revolutionary Organization (IMRO) ordered its local organizations to take quick and decisive measures in connection with the parliamentary elections. In Circular Letter No.398 dated March 20th, 1923, the Central Committee gave instructions for nominating only local honest patriots from the various parties and for their tasks after entering the National Assembly.[25] It was the only district where the Constitutional Bloc succeeded in beating the Agrarians, obtaining 36.2% and three seats out of the seven possible for the district. Two Bloc seats were gained in Vidin; one in Kyustendil; one in Plovdiv; seven in Sofia. Each one of those seats was supported by 11,922 votes.[26]

The National-Liberal Party (NLP) made its debut as a political formation in the elections of April, 1923 as well. Having united the efforts of the Liberal, both the People's Liberal and the Young Liberal—parties, it obtained 5.3% of the vote and stabilized its position, but without any seat. The National-Liberals showed a better result in the Stara Zagora district— 7.4% and in Sofia district—7.2%. In the Mastanli and Pashmakli districts they had no presence on the political scene.

Thus, at the elections in April, 1923 the BAPU strengthened its position as a prime political force, ruling the country independently, supported by more than half of those who voted and having at its disposal, by the force of the Electoral Law changes, a considerable majority in the Parliament. The Communists became the second parliamentary force again obtaining the votes of a large group of electors. The National-Liberals and the Social-Democrats did not gain any seats, having participated in the elections separately. The efforts made for building a pre-election union between the Constitutional Bloc and the BSDP in Varna, Vratza, Stara Zagora, Turnovo, Haskovo and Shoumen districts showed the results of such a decision. The Bloc of the traditional parties from the Right suffered defeat in their attempt to change the direction of political development in Bulgaria in a legal way.

The Democratic Sgovor in Power

The dramatic events in Bulgaria from the summer and autumn of 1923 led to a restoration of the dominant role of the Right in all areas of political life. The Monarch's prerogatives were also restored. A total shift of the political culture to the Right began. On the ninth of June, 1923 a successful attempt to take away the executive power from the ruling BAPU was illegally carried out. It was a putsch engineered by representatives of the Military Union and members of the People's Sgovor.

On the 10th of August, 1923 the process of consolidation of the Right was completed. The new union was called Democratic Sgovor. It was the party of the government, co-founded by the Constitutional Bloc and the People's Sgovor. The National-Liberals (unwanted by the Radical-Democrats) and the Social-Democrats, although they participated in Prof. Tzankov's cabinet, stayed out of it. From the viewpoint of tactics, the unity of the Right moved ahead as compared to the idea of consolidation of the BCP and the left wing of the BAPU in Bulgaria. This fact predetermined the further development of political processes in the country.

The attempt to exercise a Soviet-type revolution in September, 1923 was doomed from the beginning. Having successfully dealt with the revolutionary actions in some districts, having already created its own political union, the Right set new elections. The 20th National Assembly had to be replaced by a new one, as a constitutional expression of the new cabinet. Elections were necessary because there was a need to convince the world that the Bulgarian government was a legitimate one.

On the 2nd of October, 1923 an agreement for pre-election coalition between the Democratic Sgovor and the BSDP was achieved.[27] The price of bringing the Social-Democrats into the coalition was the removal from power of the National-Liberals. Their leader Smilov was forced to resign and joined the opposition. The other compromise was to yield to the

Social–Democrats' demands for more and first positions on the candidate lists. The flirtation had its risks—the BSDP managed to seize 33 such candidacies and the Democratic *Sgovor* was victorious. Having opposed so eagerly the Electoral Law changes made by the ruling BAPU on the eve of the elections for the Twentieth National Assembly, the political parties on the Right now willingly accepted the changes. They had the power; they were supposed to be the most favored.

In its pre–election campaign the government accentuated peasant democracy as the most suitable basis for political and social life in the country because peasants comprised the majority of the population. An appeal was made to the bourgeois intelligentsia to penetrate the villages and to affiliate them with the union of the social forces. The main idea of the anti–bolshevik propaganda was the thesis that in Bulgaria there were no conditions for the development of communism.[28]

In its pre–election campaign the NLP caused the government a lot of trouble, criticizing the 9th of June people from the view point of the liberal ideology. The opposition from the Left was seriously embarrassed after the failures it suffered on the 9th of June (mostly at the hands of BAPU) and again in September. Unity of action was still in the developmental process— it was incomplete and tactically behind. The BCP succeeded in certifying separate electoral lists in only three counties—the city of Rousse, Dupnitza and Eskijumaya. The BCP, the BAPU and the Craftsmen' Party registered candidate lists together in 37 counties.[29]

The pre–election preparation was dominated by the newly–formed Democratic *Sgovor*. It appealed to the entire Bulgarian population to vote for the new future of the country, against the Bolshevik violence, for unity of the nation. On the eve of the elections there were 8,472 Communists in prison; new arrests were made; publication of the Agrarians' newspaper was stopped. In some districts the united front of Communists and Agrarians was allowed to register its ballots (Pleven, Petrich, Pashmakli and Mastanli regions). Ballots were confiscated, campaign workers were removed. On the eve of the elections martial law was canceled.[30]

The election was held on the 18th of November, 1923 according to the proportional system with the changes made by the Agrarians. The government press was filled with announcements about the day of election having passed in "such exemplary order and freedom the Bulgarian voter rarely had had the chance to be pleased with".[31] One circumstance was often mentioned—as a result of the short time between the registration of lists and the day of election the candidates could not visit all the settlements in their electoral region. The population everywhere felt a great need for an explanation of the new political situation which emerged after the June putsch. The broad freedom for electoral competition had given to the opposition the ability to develop its propaganda. But the Agrarians and the Communists worked together almost everywhere. Because they were ashamed of their recent past, they did not have the courage to appear openly at public meetings. The National–Liberals used any excuse to take away, even though a small number, of votes from those given for the government list and to support if not themselves, at least the Communists and the Agrarians including, the spreading of rumors of imminent anti–Jewish pogroms on the eve of the elections.[32]

The foreign press was also in a hurry to publish news of events in the country. The Serbian newspaper *"Nishki Glasnik"* announced: "The election struggle in Bulgaria has reached its climax. The government has used every weapon at its disposal to falsify the will of the people. Instead of politicians and civilian campaigners, troops, gendarmerie and other authorities together with the Macedonians with bombs and guns are agitating among people".[33]

In comparison with the previous elections held only seven months before, on the 18th of November 1923, the number of voters who cast their ballots increased by 17,469, but in percentage there was a slight reduction of 0.3%. In general the high level of political activity had been preserved which was mostly due to compulsory voting and high taxes levied for failure to vote without valid reason. In that election 86.2% of those eligible in Bulgaria voted. There was a higher percentage of participation in the Bourgas, Pashmakli, Plovdiv and Petrich districts. But those who voted in the Rousse and Varna districts were considerably fewer in number (in the latter about 30,000 less).

The Democratic *Sgovor*–BSDP coalition gained a substantial increase in votes, in number, as well as in percent (an average of 40.8%) compared to the results of the Constitutional Bloc and the Social–Democrats obtained in spring. That could have been the result of the reduction in the number of votes for the Agrarians and the Communists. The government, of course, favored as a ruling factor, attained 58.3% of the votes. Because of the specifics of the system governing electoral law, the corresponding number of seats—201—was substantially higher. This success came as no surprise; it was expected especially after the September events and the bloody drama that followed and which had not yet been lived down by Bulgarian society.

The government coalition's strongest position was in the Petrich district (97.8% of all votes) and in the Pashmakli district (85.2%). Not a ballot had been cast there for the Agrarians or the Communists and the number of invalid ballots was small. The Petrich district continued to be anti–Agrarian, having in mind the results of the previous elections. The districts of Pashmakli and Mastanli emerged as firmly pro–government. In the spring they voted for the Agrarian government by more than 90%; in the autumn the great majority again voted for the Sgovor's ruling. Those were the districts in Bulgaria with the lowest level of literacy, 7% and 17% respectively, and a pre–dominant Bulgarian Mohammedan population which lived in small villages and hamlets spread through the country–side, very often without the simplest communications.[34]

The government received less than 50% of the votes only in the Varna and Turnovo districts (45.9% and 44.4% respectively). In those two districts the Agrarian–Communist united front coalition reached its greatest success— 45.4% in Varna and 43.0% in Turnovo.

The Agrarian–Communist bloc gained an average of 20.1% of the votes in the country. We can add to their result, not without grounds, the large number of invalid ballots (92,971 – 8.5%) because in their majority they can be considered as an indirect protest towards the government. In the slogans spread by the united Communists and Agrarians the question of protection of the interests of the working people, the perspective of worker–peasant power guaranteeing people's lives, rights and freedoms, was emphasized.

For example, in the Pleven district, popular because of the strong Agrarian influence there, the number of invalid ballots was 23,851, or 24.9% of all votes, and in the Bourgas district 22.7% voted in this way. Here is the explanation of the forces on the Left for the results, as written by the ruling formation newspaper: "The elections ... show that a consider-able number of our people have not been cured of the agrarian and communist pest yet. The substantial successes of the united Agrarians and Communists indicate how great is the danger coming from them and that this danger has not been completely removed. The unity achieved between the democratic forces in the country by the creation of the Democratic Sgovor should be preserved at any cost. The results show no party could separately by itself protect the country from this enormous evil."[35]

Having left the cabinet, Smilov sent in his resignation on the 22nd of September, 1923 not without the interference of the Social–Democrats, the

National–Liberals took part in the elections as opposition again. The green ballot was cast by 11.0% of the voters. After unscrupulous propaganda and criticism of the Right and the Left, the Liberals obtained their greatest success in parliamentary elections after the wars. The liberal party *Narodno Edinstvo* led by Dr.Genadiev took part separately and gained a modest 0.4%. The Kyustendil district strengthened its position as the liberal "fortress" in the country (from 16% in spring to 17.7% on the 18th of September, 1923). The Liberals from the Plovdiv and Vratza districts continued to obtain their same good results (17.3% and 15.9%).[36]

The places in the new National Assembly were distributed according to the Electoral Law without real correspondence to the political influence and people's will: for the ruling coalition—201 seats, of which 56 were Democrats, 42 from the People's *Sgovor,* 41 for the UCPP, 32 for the Radicals and 30 for the Social–Democrats. Participating in the Sgovorist coalition, the Radicals and the Socialists took more seats than if they had participated separately. The BCP and the BAPU were represented by 38 deputies (9 Communists and 29 Agrarians) and the National–Liberals by 8.

Professor Tzankov, the prime–minister, managed to realize his goal— the government had at last been legalized at home and legitimized abroad.[37]

The Sgovor *Against Its Alternative*

Until the end of the 1920's, the parties and groups from the Right dominated the political reality in Bulgaria. The most significant and most active among them were co–ruling in the coalition of the Democratic Sgovor. Then, however, the struggle between the two wings in the Sgovor strengthened. Those were the wings of the moderate Right and the reactionary authoritarian. The inner erosion of the 9th of June's regime and its political system led to the appearance of a new element in political life. Parliamentary opposition to the regime from the Right emerged within the Democratic Party, the Radical Party, the National–Liberal Party etc. It had existed since 1924 as a political alternative oriented to the Right and from now on it would unite and prevail as a factor in political life.

Other groups of Sgovorists also separated from the Democratic *Sgovor* and following the example of Italy, founded a few pro–fascist formations like the political circle "*Zveno*", Bulgarian National Association, Union of the Bulgarian Fascists. They were authoritarian, revisionistic and, above all, parties without any significant popularity in society and without a solid social basis.

Nor could the Macedonian organization (IMRO) avoid the decaying processes. The disagreement among its leaders led to a series of murders. Fear paralyzed normal political and social life especially in the Petrich region. For the parliamentary elections in 1927, the IMRO enforced the so-called List on the entire community including local names. All those who participated cast their ballots for it.

For a period of time the Social-Democrats collaborated with the cabinet, but in the spring of 1924, they undertook a separate line of political behavior. The Socialists were losing more and more of their prestige and influence in the political system, as well as among their previous followers.

From the middle of the 1920's a complicated process of re-grouping among the Agrarians had been in progress. In 1926, the BAPU split into BAPU–"1 *Vrabcha*" and BAPU "Orange". Thousands of BAPU's supporters stood behind them. Later a number of various Agrarian groups appeared.

In 1924 the Law for State Defense was passed signaling the start of extraordinary legislation. It prohibited the BCP's presence in Bulgarian political life, pursuing and punishing severely any act of the Communist party which had been proclaimed to be a terrorist organization. The tragic events in 1923-1924 reached their climax after the outrage in Sofia's St.Nedelya cathedral in April, 1925.* The BCP went underground but succeeded in creating its legal form of existence at the beginning of 1927, immediately prior to the next regular parliamentary elections. The name of this new leftist organization was the Bulgarian Workers' Party (BWP).

By the end of 1927 there were 2,399 organizations in Bulgaria. Of them 21 were political (excluding the BCP, the BCYU and the organizations for national liberty); 321 were professional; 1663 cultural-educational and 475 for physical training.[38]

On the 4th of January, 1926 Tzankov's cabinet tendered its resignation and a new government was formed led by Andrei Lyapchev, a representative of the traditional-party tendency in the Sgovor. The change of the cabinets was brought about by the need for a new personality not associated with the repressions and the bloody nightmares of the past and by the inner erosion of the ruling coalition. The Prime Minister's popular phrase, said in a slight Macedonian dialect, contained the new slogan: "Gently, with good!".

---

* The BCP plotted to murder many ministers, deputies and military officers who would attend the funeral of a general killed a few days earlier by the Communists.

The date for parliamentary elections for the Twenty–Second National Assembly was fixed for the 29th of May, 1927. The political forces preparing to participate were the ruling Democratic *Sgovor* (which reached an agreement with the National–Liberals Stambolovists for a local coalition in some places), the so–called Lead Coalition (a pre–election union between the BAPU–G.Markov, the BSDP and the Craftsmen' Party), the Triple Coalition (including the Democratic Party, the National–Liberal Party Kyorchev and the BAPU–K.Tomov), the pre–election union of the RDP and the Agrarians–Dragievists, the Workers' Party etc.

The opposition press spoke loudly and extensively about the government terror and arbitrariness which was occurring everywhere. The police organized bands and disrupted the opposition meetings even in the capital. Campaigners from the opposition of the Right, as well as of the Workers' party were beaten. The *"Zname"* newspaper edited by the separated Democrats wrote on the 21st of May, 1927: "Being afraid they may lose the elections, the Sgovorists simply have lost their minds."

On the 22nd of May, 1927 the parties in the Triple Coalition approached the Bulgarian voters with an appeal.[40] It said that Bulgaria's present rulers still held the power having taken it four years ago by means of a putsch; the change of government was necessary and it should be done. There was an appeal for the unity of social forces affirming that the parties already had this thought in mind. The coalition's tasks were defined as follows: change of government, pacification of the country, removal of the citizens' lack of trust in the state, and social unity for a ruling body supported by the people. Three slogans of the Triple Coalition appeared: "Down with the fronts!" (against the class hatred); "Down with the hatreds!" (the competition of ideas should serve for creative work, not for destruction) and "Long live the law regime!" (there is not a legal state without equality before the law).[41]

On the 29th of May, 1927, 84.2% of the eligible men cast their ballots. They numbered 1,183,122 – 86,650 more than in 1923 but 1.9% less.[42]

The Democratic *Sgovor* obtained separately 35.0% and in coalition with the National–Liberal Party (Stambolov) 9.1% of the vote. It was the average for the country and presented an obvious retreat from the result registered in November 1923. Their strongest positions were again in the Pashmakli district (perhaps because they were still the ruling)—71.2% and a comparatively good presentation in Rousse district—55.5%.[43] The greatest loss of influence suffered by the ruling party formation was in the Vratza and Kyustendil districts. The election results show that votes previously cast for the *Sgovor* had gone to the new coalitions. In those coalitions, parties having separated from the Sgovorist rule united with strong wings of the Agrarian movement.

The Lead Coalition was in second place in its political influence, having received 285,758 votes, or an average of 24.1% for the country. In the Turnovo and Kyustendil districts the coalition obtained nearly 40% of the votes which was a considerable success. This was due to the traditionally strong position of the Agrarians and the Social–Democrats in Turnovo and to the weakening of the *Sgovor*'s position in Kyustendil. The Lead Coalition was very weak organizationally in the Mastanli and Pashmakli districts with only 5.2% and 9.6% in those districts.[44]

The other coalition—called the Triple—occupied third place with its election results of a country–wide average of 15.1%. Only in the Vidin, Mastanli and Sofia districts did the Triple Coalition succeed in winning over the Lead, mostly because of the strong influence that the DP had in those regions. In the Varna, Vratza, Vidin, Kyustendil and Turnovo districts the united efforts of both coalitions would have been successful if they had acted together against the Sgovorists.[45]

The remaining parties and pre–election unions were not successful in achieving any substantial result. The Radicals–Dragievists presented themselves in a rather mediocre way—2.5%—which was the proof of their weak popularity. The remaining part of the NLP, except the Stambolovists and the Kyorchevists, suffered a full defeat gaining only 1.6% of the vote, although they had a stronger influence in the town of Sofia—11% of the votes.

In May, 1927 the BCP declared its position towards the coalitions participating in the elections. The Triple Coalition was classified as "a bourgeois opposition" which was directed against the fascist character of the Democratic *Sgovor*'s government; as "a bourgeois reserve of the politically bankrupted *Sgovor*'s regime". The Communists became jealous of the Lead Coalition (the "Iron" Bloc of Labor) considering it to be a serious crack in the common labor front and "a strike in the back of the fighting masses of people in front of the face of their common raging enemy".[46]

The Workers' Party, still having not been very popular under this name, obtained the votes of only 2.5% of those who voted, or 29,210 in number. It had a greater success in Sofia—19.3%—and its weakest showing was in the Turnovo, Vratza and Rousse districts.[47]

It was only in the Petrich district that the election was held in a different way. A list "of the entire community" (Macedonian group) was registered there and in fact the election was carried out under the thumb of the IMRO. All the valid ballots cast were in favor of this list—37,854 in number, or 3.3% of the vote in Bulgaria.

The results of the parliamentary elections in 1927 indicated again the preponderance of those forces connected with the Democratic *Sgovor* and the ruling circles although the figures were now much lower in comparison with November, 1923. The opposition press affirmed that in all the biggest towns where the government could not act with impunity, the opposition gained the overwhelming majority of votes. It was mostly characteristic of Sofia where society kept a close eye on the government, the level of education was higher and the population was better informed. In the capital, of 11 seats the government succeeded in getting only four. "*Zname*", the newspaper of the DP, very seriously turned the attention of the people to the activity in the rural areas where only careful planning could lead to results as good as those in the big towns.[48]

The Government press, in turn, came to another conclusion—the Bolshevik agents in Bulgaria had again started weaving their webs. In towns like Radomir and Kyustendil, where after the September and April events the Communists had seemingly disappeared, they now gained a considerable number of votes. The country's first resort area, the town of Varna, had fallen into the Communists' hands and in the capital they had obtained more deputy seats than all other opposition parties. Unity of action between the Communists and the Agrarians from BAPU–Vrabcha could be observed everywhere, even the closest advisor of K.Muraviev, one of the Agrarian leaders, was called "a Communist fox".[49]

The effort of the moderate group on the Right, which had separated from the Sgovorist formation and had become its alternative, to form a coalition with the National–Liberals and the Agrarians did not succeed in its final goal—to change the government. However it showed that was the proper way to remove the extreme Right from power.

The Triumph of Choice

In the years that followed the last parliamentary elections in 1927, Bulgaria, as well as the whole world, entered a period of economic crisis. In the political arena the second Sgovorist cabinet led by Lyapchev continued to rule the country. During the cabinet crisis in the spring of 1931 negotiations were even held with Alexander Malinov—one of the Rightist opposition leaders. The variety of political parties, formations and organizations continued to grow. On the eve of the following parliamentary elections there was a tendency toward compromise with a single goal—unity. The revolutionary communist movement was paralyzed in a narrow class political frame which limited its influence among the different social groups and isolated it from the other anti-Sgovorist democratic forces because of its direct dependence on the Communist international organization. The inner crisis in the National-Liberation movement deepened, but it could not be neglected when estimating political reality, especially in the south-western part of Bulgaria.

The name of the new political phenomenon, People's Bloc, quickly became a factor of paramount significance. The People's Bloc was founded on the eve of the elections of the Twenty-Third National Assembly held on the 30th of May, 1931. After a period of long and rather difficult negotiations between the opposition parties the new coalition united the forces of the DP, the BAPU-*Vrabcha*, a wing of the NLP, the RDP (which made a compromise with the understanding it never would participate in a union with the Stambolovists) and the BAPU-*Stara Zagora* (the latter later left the new union). The leading factor was the DP. In early June, 1931 some of the leaders and many local organizations of the BAPU "Orange" supported the new coalition. Thus the People's Bloc was formed as an opposition concentration of political parties from the Right and most of the Agrarian organizations. The leading factor was the Democratic party. This provided wide support for the Bloc at the elections and to a great extent predetermined its success.

The pre-election platform of the Bloc was accepted on the 9th of June, 1931 after a long period of disagreement and discussion on specific points of the document, on the party political structure of the future power and even on the election color of the coalition (the Democrats insisted on the purple and the Agrarians on their lemon-yellow). The platform was widely spread in pre-election press materials like the "Manifest to the Bulgarian people". Its main ideas were: protection of the Turnovo Constitution; the overthrow of the *Sgovor* government and establishment of a new people's power; recovery of the national economy and protection of the economically weak working people; a policy of peace and good will with Bulgaria's neighbors and with the rest of the world.[50]

The People's Bloc directed its campaign to the urban citizens and the peasants, the workers, the craftsmen, the merchants and the officials, appealing to them to cast the purple ballot. The "orange" Agrarians published an appeal to their followers to vote for the People's Bloc. The craftsmen's group, with the Sofia town Democratic organization, published a leaflet directed to the craftsmen confirming that the People's Bloc platform was a full reflection of their interests.[51]

Another pre–election coalition was the Peasant National Bloc uniting the Liberal–Radoslavists around the "*Narodni prava*" newspaper and a part of the Agrarians from the BAPU–*Vrabcha*. That Bloc declared its support of a policy of peace and peace treaty revision using non–military means; protection of state order; law and order and relief through a common amnesty for political crimes and the removal of the abuse of the Law for protection of the state and for agrarian reforms. That coalition appealed for a struggle against the conservative *Sgovor*, for people's national power by the cooperation of all creative forces and working classes in Bulgaria, to a "silent by idea and by object coalition" of the opposition forces with a single goal—to defeat the government. However, on the 20th of June the propaganda was directed against Malinov, too, who they said had reached a secret agreement with Lyapchev to save the *Sgovor* from defeat.[52]

The Workers' Party also united in a pre–election union with the Agrarians on the Left forming the Bloc of Labor. It relied on the support and votes of the socially weakest class, the workers and the small farm owners. The Sofia correspondent of the Berlin *Internationale* newspaper listed the participants in this new Bloc of Labor in his report in May, 1931: "the legal class–conscious workers' party in the same front from below with the Agrarians on the Left, the representatives of the refugees, the indepen- dent trade unions and the plain village poverty" led by the BCP.[53]

The elections for the Twenty–third National Assembly were held on the 21st of June, 1931 and present one of the few cases in the electoral history of Bulgaria when the ruling party lost the election. 1,315,507 people voted, or 85.2% of those who were eligible according to the lists. This showed a slight increase in voter participation—about 1%—compared to 1927. The most active were the electors from the Mastanli district (90.2%), Vratza (89.6%) and Vidin (89%). The least number of participants was in Turnovo (75.7%), Haskovo (79.7%) and in Sofia where it barely reached 74.7%.[54]

The results showed a further decrease in popularity of the ruling Democratic *Sgovor*. Their average result for the country was 30.6%. The *Sgovor* gained its greatest success in the Mastanli district—58.8%, but in seven districts it could not reach the 30% mark. As compared to the previous elections the government lost 118,906 votes, or 13.5%.

The great success of the People's Bloc was the 47.5% of the vote of all participants in accordance with the clauses of the electoral system, which ensured 150 of the 274 places in the Assembly. The Bloc won a glorious victory in the Vidin (59%) and Kyustendil (57%) districts. The Pashmakli district was again on the side of the winner, as the Bloc took 62% of the votes. Comparatively low was the result in the Mastanli district (36%) and in the Petrich district where no one voted for this political force.

The Peasant–National Bloc of Liberals and Agrarians showed weak results and hardly achieved 0.3% of the votes. The failure was explained by the "hypnosis" to which the opposition voters were exposed by the People's Bloc propaganda in everyday newspapers.[55]

The Bloc of Labor results showed the high popularity of the Workers' Party. Together with the Agrarians on the Left and supported by some refugees representatives and the trade unions it obtained 12.7% or 167,281 votes. It was only in the Mastanli and Petrich districts that the Bloc of Labor did not participate (in the latter the votes went to the Socialist Federation candidates). It achieved traditionally good result in the Bourgas district (20.4%) and in the Haskovo district (18.7%). In the capital, 19.2% voted in favor of the Bloc of Labor and again confirmed the fears about the popularity of the Left in Sofia. The Bloc of Labor was successful in the big industrial towns and in some large villages. The communist pre–election slogans were: "Down with the fascist dictatorship!"," Long live the workers' and peasants' government!"," Down with Lyapchev, Tzankov, Malinov and Company with their fascist people's bloc and people's coalition!", "To defend the USSR till our death!"," Long live the Balkan federation of workers' and peasants' republics!". The Workers' Party won 32 seats in the National Assembly.[56]

The Social–Democrats participated separately in the election and registered a decrease in their relative weight in the political life of the country. The BSDP won 27,323 votes and took five seats in the National

Assembly. The Petrich region again sent eight deputies to the Parliament. Only 79 places from all the districts remained for the government then in power in the Parliament.

The parliamentary elections in 1931 present an extremely important element in modern Bulgarian history. The people's vote forced the government to submit its resignation. In fact that was the end of the *Sgovor*'s eight years of rule. The coalition of the moderate Right together with the wide Agrarian circles won. Its pre-election platform was trans-formed into the government program of the new cabinet led by Al.Malinov.

The pro-government press bitterly noted that the cabinet lost for many reasons—mostly because of the economic crisis, because the long term of the *Sgovor*'s rule blunted the government and had created a mood for change among the people and because the *Sgovor* lost some deputy seats in the country.[57] In a statement of the ex-prime-minister, Lyapchev, given to the press, he said that the result was not bad because it removed a conviction spread abroad that in Bulgaria the elections were always in favor of the government and our people were an amorphous mass. In order to obtain the successful result the People's Bloc had to unite four oppositional parties.[58]

Bulgaria was seized with hope for democratization of political life and economic reforms.

On the Road to a Coup D'Etat

After the People's Bloc victory and the *Sgovor*'s loss of power the process of political division accelerated in the country. The ruling coalition itself was not a stable political concentration; it was constantly torn by internal arguments between the partners because of their unequal positions in the union.

The Democratic Party, the leading force in the Bloc, had at its disposal 42 seats in the parliament, and in the government the post of Prime Minister (Malinov, then Mushanov), the Ministry of the Interior, the Ministry of Foreign Affairs and the Finance Ministry. The BAPU-*Vrabcha*, the strongest wing of the Agrarian Union held 70 seats in the Assembly and three ministries in the government. The NLP (D.Vurbenov) which was rather unstable, had 24 seats and two ministries, those of Education and of Justice. The RDP (St.Kosturkov) was the weakest partner in the Bloc. It held nine seats in the Parliament and its leader, Kosturkov, was the Railway Minister.[59]

The People's Bloc government did not fulfil its program. Having been elected as an alternative to the Democratic *Sgovor* its main task was to strengthen the parliamentary constitutional system following the Turnovo Constitution. It became impossible in view of the world–wide economic crisis to fulfil their task in the area of economic recovery. The People's Bloc was exposed to the criticism of many political forces—the BCP, the opposition wings of the NLP, a part of the Democratic *Sgovor* led by Lyapchev and Bourov and another part of the *Sgovor* separated in 1932 and led by Professor Tzankov who established the National Socialist Movement, the Secret Military Union, the political circle *"Zveno"* etc. The so–called "irresponsible factors" of the terrorist IMRO were hostile as well.

Beginning in 1933 and early 1934 some groups and formations refuting the parliamentary system strengthened their positions and their appetite for power. They criticized the parties as nets of factious struggle and guilty for the economic crisis. At the head of list was the NSM led by Tzankov characterized as the best organized and as the party having the most members who embraced fascist ideas. The development of the political circle *"Zveno"* was of substantial importance for it appealed to a non–party form of state organization as well. The Secret Military Union led by Damyan Velchev and directly connected to the *"Zveno"* had already been preparing a violent change of government.

On the 19th of May, 1934, the Military Union, supported politically by the *"Zveno"* led by Kimon Georgiev, engineered a successful coup d'etat and a dictatorship was established in the country. The coup d'etat was carried out directly against the People's Bloc government. However, it soon became clear that it swept up a whole variety of political parties and small groups declaring them to be unlawful. The purpose was the complete liquidation of the political party system in Bulgaria.

CHAPTER IV
1934-1946: FROM NON-PARTY TO ONE PARTY SYSTEM

The Three Political Tendencies

By the end of 1935 the political development of the country could be clearly distinguished by three major tendencies. The first, reactionary, disposed to dictatorship and authoritarian rule, was at the helm of state power. It was supported by the Palace, the Military Union, the NSM and other similar organizations, created after the fashion of the fascist party in Italy – SZO, SBNL, Ratnik, etc. The second trend developing in Bulgarian political life was the democratic-liberal, whose course was forcibly halted with the coup on May 19, 1934. Its followers were representatives of the former, now dissolved, right-wing and center political parties. Most significant among them, as before, were the DP and the BAPU, again having irreconcilable differences. The third political tendency was the revolutionary one on the Left, supported by the BCP, the BAPU left-wing groups and the BSDP and others experiencing an evolution.

On the further independent development of these tendencies, on the complex interrelations between them and on their struggle for predominance depended the destiny of the country. From a policy of total neutrality Bulgaria would join the fascist Axis (under the dominating role of the reactionaries). Later an attempt would be made to divert the state from the orbit of a satellite (second tendency) and still later it would take part in the War against its former allies with the clear intention of a close commitment with the Soviet Union (the third revolutionary trend from the Left became dominant in the political life).

The first attempt at unification of the non-fascist forces came from the democratic-liberal group—the formation of the so called Five (May 24, 1936) by the BAPU-Vrabtcha 1, the Democratic Sgovor-Lyaptchev, the NLP of B. Smilov-D. Varbanov, the right-wing of the BWSDP around Kr. Pastuhov and the RDP of Prof. G. P. Genov. In a memorandum sent to the King they demanded immediate restoration of civil political rights, because the Turnovo Constitution had been suspended, formation of a responsible

71

government (probably amidst the Five) and a return to a normal parliamentary life, i.e. Parliamentary elections.

Due to their irreconcilable differences with the BAPU, the DP stayed out of this union. The platform of the Five was co–ordinated at the end of December, 1936. For its preparation some agreement was reached with the DP and RP. "The nationwide request" united the aspirations of all non–fascist democratic groups in Bulgarian society for restoration of democratic civil rights, as laid down in the Constitution. The establishment of constitutional committees in support of the "nationwide request" began in February, 1937. The first of them was established in Varna on January 18, 1937 with the participation of all democratic parties and the BCP.

In the second ten days of January, 1937 an agreement between the Five, the RP, the DP and the BAPU–Pladne (the group of G. M. Dimitrov) was reached for cooperation in the forthcoming elections. For the first time in the political life of the country efforts of such a wide circle of political parties were united. Their tactic was to cast a ballot–paper with an inscription reading, "The Turnovo Constitution to be restored!". According to the official information of the day, at the election, which was held in March, 1937 by counties consecutively, not simultaneously, about 22% of the participants voted by slogans. Those who dared to vote against the regime in the towns were much greater in numbers than in the villages (25% against 19%). The result in Sofia was 58.37% in favor of the opposition and 41.63% for the Government. In some places in the regions of Shoumen, Pleven and Vratza the Democratic Union even won a victory.[1] This comparatively low percentage won by the Five and the other parties was due to a certain extent to the fact that the candidates for municipal councilors nominated by the authorities were former partisans of the same parties. People knew them as such and voted for them, not quite convinced by the tactics of boycott. The municipal elections in 1937 were a dress rehearsal for the forthcoming Parliamentary elections, which were to be held after a pause of seven years.

Majority System Again

Kioseivanov's second Government took some steps to determine what the real influence of the former so–called "parties of the order" was among the people, the popularity of their leaders and the eventual results in future elections. The Prime Minister was not alien to the idea still not very well clarified, of involving some of the former partisans in the government, in order to give it a more democratic appearance.

The information from a survey carried out by the Ministry of Internal Affairs on the political disposition of the people in the summer of 1936 was indicative. There was a firm general wish of the people that the party regime be restored to power. Some organization was evident only among the Communists, the NSD and the Agrarians and in the county of Sofia among the Democrats, the Democratic *Sgovor* and the group that carried out the coup on the 19th of May. A Report of the Department of Police titled "The disposition of the masses according to the reports of the county police inspectors" examined the predominant dispositions in the different regions and found that in Bourgas it was mainly to the Left; in Vratza disbelief and a bigger interest in the Agrarian Union; in Plovdiv, a strong influence of the NSD even among the non–party people and transition of supporters from the Workers' Party to Tzankov. In Pleven— disposition in the BAPU, WP and Democrats was favored and in Sofia—all former parties. In Stara Zagora there was a negative disposition to all parties; in Shumen, again negative, but if the Electoral Law were not adjusted, the people might vote again for the former parties.

The question of eventual grouping in future elections in the counties was also investigated. Although subjective, the police survey showed that by September–October 1936, the political parties were still powerful and that the Government could hardly expect to be successful in new elections. That is why they were postponed.[2]

After the October 22, 1937 test with the municipal elections, a decree was published for the carrying out of Parliamentary elections. According to the new law, in contradiction to the Constitution, the number of deputies was reduced from 274 to 160. The electoral colleges were formed according to the will and taste of the Government with 20,000 to 40,000 votes. The majority system was established again. A candidate had personally to declare his candidacy; there was an explicit interdiction for the political affiliation of the candidates. Ministers could not become deputies and vice versa. In the colleges with only one candidate approved by the Court no elections were envisaged—the candidate was simply pronounced "elected". By this decree, for the first time in the Parliamentary history of Bulgaria women were given the right to vote (although partially). The franchise was given to those who were married, divorced or widowed, but they could not be elected.[3] For this part of the electorate participation was not obligatory. No election rights were given to military officers, soldiers, policemen or customs officers. The future Parliament had to legislate obediently under the baton of the King and the Government he had appointed.

The new Electoral Law was not accepted with much enthusiasm. The population, especially in the mountain regions, expressed some discontent in relation to the right given to women to vote, as a completely inexplicable condition with regard to "the strength of our oligarchic traditions". The discontent and disappointment could also be felt among the population in those places where the weather had devastated agriculture for years. Some candidates would be unable to participate owing to their unpaid taxes. The reaction in the headquarters of the former parties in the cities was spontaneous and abrupt, due to the fact that the law eliminated the possibility of political parties taking part as party formations. Thus the decision to call upon the electors to vote with slogans. After the authorities announced the punitive sanctions for voting with slogans, the tactics were changed—boycott the election or drop empty envelopes in the ballot-boxes. All political parties without exception declared the new Electoral Law to be extremely reactionary, drastic and medieval. The restrictions were considered to be chains preventing the free expression of the will of the people.[4]

During his visit and meetings in Rousse in 1937, Poisson, the eminent French figure of the co-operative movement, suggested the establishment of a united front of all political parties— "defenders of democracy" in Bulgaria. This idea was adopted and in the end of November of the same year, in Rousse, the Constitutional Block with representatives of all parties excluding Tzankov's NSD was established. An Appeal addressed to the leaders of all parties in Sofia was prepared and signed, urging them to widen the front all over Bulgaria. A notice of the event and quotations from the Appeal were published in the French magazine "Voix Européene" No. 23-24, 1937 December.[5]

A central agreement for common action in the elections between the Five, the DP, the RDP of St. Kosturkov, the BAPU-Pladne and the BCP was reached at the end of January or in the beginning of February, 1938. The new coalition was called Democratic Union or Constitutional Block. The pre-election platform was very democratic—restoration of the Turnovo Constitution, income tax, ensuring free markets, every peasant family to be granted some minimum acreage of arable land. This program was published in the USA and in France.[6]

The period before the elections was accompanied by total pre–election terror—arrests, interference in pre–election meetings, interdiction of all opposition political propaganda. The successful methods used in the municipal elections were employed once again.[7]

There were reasons for the restlessness of the authorities. In many reports of the county police chiefs the dangerous influence of the travelling campaigners of the "People's Front" was emphasized. They visited small towns, especially the villages, as merchants, commissioners, etc., met openly and secretly with former party functionaries and explained the building–up of the People's Front election committees. Most zealous in this pre–election campaign were the Communists and the Agrarians–followers of Gitchev.[8]

The reaction of the authorities was quick and to the point—as early as January, 1938 the county directors were asked by cable if they are ready and whether they could hit the Communist Party and its branches with enough evidence for the Court. In the days till the election, police managers all over the country were contesting in Court the candidacies of those, who were suspected of being partisans of the former political parties.[9]

The elections were held on March 6 in the counties of Shoumen and Stara Zagora, on March 13 in Pleven and Bourgas, on March 20 in Vratza and Plovdiv and on March 27 in Sofia. In these elections 2,198,831 electors or 69.5% of all people who could vote took part. Most active was the electorate in the counties of Shoumen and Bourgas, most feeble was the participation in the county of Plovdiv. Less than half of the women (49.5%), given the right to vote for the first time, cast their ballots. The 50% of women's participation was surpassed in the counties with the highest voting percentage in general—Bourgas and Shoumen. It was lowest in the county of Stara Zagora. Again the rural constituencies were more active than those in the towns, but now the difference was substantially smaller—1.7%. It was only in the county of Sofia that the number of those who voted from the towns exceeded the participation of the farming communities.[10] In the capital city mass participation of the women occurred, partly because many of the candidates had come out with special appeals to the women voters.[11]

Owing to the articles of the Electoral Law (the explicit interdiction against taking part or campaigning on behalf of a political party) a profound analysis of the results from the elections turned out to be difficult. A more precise picture of the political preferences and feelings based on the number of votes for those who were elected and those candidates who were defeated can be given only for the county of Shoumen. *(See Table 1, page 125)*

Political Disposition of the Shoumen District Population
According to the Electoral Results in March, 1938

Party affiliation of candidates	Votes	% of the vote	Seats
NSD	38,778	10.4	1
Sgovor–Lyapchev	49,153	13.2	3
NLP	20,832	5.6	1
DP	37,473	10.1	4
RDP	1,745	0.5	–
"Zveno"	1,497	0.4	–
BSDP	12,175	3.3	2
BAPU	28,837	7.7	2
BAPU–Vrabcha 1	77,755	20.9	6
BAPU–Pladne	46,567	12.5	–
BWP	2,434	0.6	–
Non–party	48,951	13.1	5

AMVR, ob 1782, T. I, 1.29–31; T.II, 1.154.

In the country as a whole, there was a total of 940,706 votes for the elected candidates, 582,596 for the government candidates and 358,110 for the opposition.[12] The majority system established by the Electoral Law and the great number of candidates, who split the votes, were the reasons for more than half of the voters not having representatives in the Parliament.

Only in the county of Stara Zagora did the Democratic Union win over the government candidates, taking 11 out of 21 seats. The opposition achieved success in the major cities—Plovdiv, Turnovo, Sliven, Bourgas and Stara Zagora. In Sofia, where the headquarters of the parties and the management of the Democratic Union were situated it won all nine seats. Most of the opposition leaders lived in those cities and thus were in a better position to actively participate in the pre–election campaign in areas where the population was better informed and more literate.[13]

The reverse was true in the regions of the Rhodopi Mountains and in Ludogorie where there was lower degree of education and understanding of political reality; it was much easier for the authorities to resort to terror tactics and pre–election pressure; to turn to repression in order to gain success. These regional peculiarities were recognized and used by the ruling powers when establishing the constituencies.

The Government won 96 seats, the opposition 64, a result which was inadequate and would soon bring insecurity within the Parliament. The police reported the main reasons for the unsuccessful management of the election campaign in some constituencies were: (1) the cohesion of the "front on the Left" and the lack of a union between "the Right–wing" (2) insufficient cooperation on behalf of the police forces (3) the ruinous activity of the co–operatives and the *tchitalishta* (library clubs) (4) the lack of interest on behalf of the officials from other ministries except the Ministry of the Interior and (5) "the liberty, which was given at the elections and was not appropriate for the time".[14]

The opposition would have claims on Parliamentary control, mainly in the sphere of foreign policy. In accordance with their former party affiliations, the opposition Parliamentary group was as follows: NSM – 3 (Al. Tzankov was elected in Sofia); from the Democratic Union – 56; others – 4. The make–up of the deputies of the Democratic Union was quite interesting. All participating parties won seats, half of them by the BAPU–Vrabtcha 1, followed by the BAPU–Pladne. The BCP, in spite of their claims of broad influence among the working classes had only five seats, the BSDP – eight and the DP – only one.[15] In the new Twenty–fourth National Assembly the major political parties from the recent past were present. Only the until recently ruling Political Club "Zveno" had no deputies.

In spite of the massive propaganda in favor of non–party rule, the majority of the elected government deputies (86) had been members of different parties in the past. This was the reason why the definition "affiliated with today's authority" was often used. Only ten had never been party members. As a matter of fact, in the election contest "the party of the Government" competed against the parties of the opposition. In that sense "the non–party structure" of the regime had become "party structure", personified by the use of "affiliated" by the Government candidates. The electorate had to choose between "the affiliated" who were often connected with their former party membership and the opposition candidates.

Nevertheless, the existence of this opportunity predetermined the presence of the opposition's future in the Parliament. The party of "the affiliated" had have a majority, not for legislation and Parliamentary control, but to legitimize the Government and to give a constitutional character to the ruling monarchy.

The participation of the Democratic Union in the elections for the Twenty–fourth National Assembly and their results were a success. The unification of the efforts of the democratic–liberal and the revolutionary–left–wing tendencies in Bulgarian political life which centered on the idea of restoration of constitutional civil rights was proved to be a necessity. The election results demonstrated the considerable leveling of the influence of both tendencies among the population. The Agrarian groups still had a strong and convincing presence, but at the same time the influence of the DP and NLP was reduced.

The Democratic Union from 1938 was the last and only agreement achieved with such a wide spectrum of political parties in Bulgaria. The consensus reached on the idea for restoration of the Turnovo Constitution united in the pre–election campaign former Radicals and People's Liberals, Communists and members of the Democratic *Sgovor*, Democrats and Agrarians. Nevertheless, the victory, although incomplete, was for the Government.

Elections in the Beginning of the War

In the summer of 1939 it became evident that with this structure of the National Assembly the executive power would not be able to manoeuvre without hindrance. The complex international conditions—the unsuccessful negotiations in Moscow between Great Britain, France and the USSR, the conclusion of the Ribbentrop–Molotov Pact and especially the beginning of the war in Europe—accelerated. The Twenty–fourth National Assembly, which had existed for little more than a year faced a crisis; it was forced to adjourn before the end of the term and to set elections for the Twenty–fifth National Assembly. The aspiration was to eliminate not only the counter-action of the opposition deputies, but also the wish for Parliamentary control that appeared among a part of the Parliamentary majority surrounding the Chairman of the National Assembly, Stoitcho Moshanov, and the Chairman of the Parliamentary Commission for foreign affairs, Govedarov.

The new elections were again fixed for four different Sundays: December 24, 1939 in the county of Shumen; January 14, 1940 in the counties of Bourgas and Pleven; the 21st of January in Vratza and Plovdiv and the 28th of January in Sofia and Stara Zagora. The aim was to hold elections first in those counties where was envisaged success for the Government and the result would then affect the elections in the remaining counties. That was the reason the county of Stara Zagora (the only place the opposition had won in the elections for the Twenty-fourth National Assembly in 1938) was to be the last, together with the capital city Sofia, where the opposition was strongest.

The instructions of the Electoral Decree imposed too many obstacles and complications on the nomination of candidates, particularly with the requirement for declarations which included denial of all anti-state ideas—anarchic, communist and other violent methods of struggle as well as party membership, were geared to the success of the Government. This forced many party leaders to give up their party memberships on the eve of or during the elections, and to affiliate with the Government. In its favor is the fact that the Government did not repeat the mistake from the elections for the Twenty-fourth National Assembly. In that case only one Government candidate, with almost no exceptions, was nominated in each constituency, to avoid splitting of votes and eventual failure. There were 162 government candidates competing in 160 constituencies.[16]

In comparison with 1938, the opposition was unprepared, adrift and confused, disturbed by developments in the international situation. The democratic-liberal opposition with its traditional sympathies to Great Britain and France, did not approve the non-aggression Treaty signed between Germany and the Soviet Union, and repudiated the aggression in Poland. This predetermined its future co-operation in the pre-election campaign with the Worker's Party which had begun negotiations for unity but soon, under the influence of the Comintern was discouraged from doing so because of instructions to establish the united front without the participation of democratic and social-democratic leaders. Nevertheless an agreement was reached between the Worker's Party, the BAPU-Vrabtcha 1 and the BAPU-Pladne and Zveno. Some Social-Democrats also supported the agreement, although they did not share the evaluation of the WP that the war was "imperialistic". The agreement was based up on the appeal for the power of the people, for peace and for a treaty which would ensure eternal friendship with the USSR. Owing to the tendency to impose some

candidates from the WP and other parties, unity was not achieved every—
where. Candidates of the United Front were registered in 120 constituencies,
but what is more important—only in 64 constituencies were there common
candidates. In the remaining 56 candidates were nominated without
pre—arrangement which led to the splitting of votes.[17]

In its pre—election propaganda the Government emphasized the
positive moments of the non—party rule, which saved the country from
meaningless partisan passions. The need for peace and the preservation of
Bulgarian neutrality in the war that was already consuming Europe was
pointed out. A very interesting element was the recently emerged, "pro—
soviet" disposition of the ruling circles. The government candidates were
favorably disposed to "Slav Russia" in their pre—election meetings with the
electors, assisted by the Government's extension of the commercial and
cultural relationships with the USSR. In that respect the manifestation of
some tolerance for the pre—election slogans of the WP, on behalf of the
authorities, should be noted. To appeal for the signing of a treaty for
friendship with the Soviet Union prior to the 23rd of August, 1939 was
dangerous and punishable. In this pre—election campaign, the police "closed
their eyes" to such declarations.

In the elections held in the end of 1939 and in the beginning of
1940, 67.2% of the electorate took part. This represented a small reduction
in the activity of the voters. The number of women that voted was decreased
substantially, especially in the county of Sofia (from 49.3 to 37.8%). Most
active was the participation of the voters in the county of Stara Zagora,
despite its withdrawal on the last day of the election (89.5% for men and
49.9% for women). The political activity of the electorate in the towns fell
considerably, while in the villages it remained almost the same in compari—
son with 1938.[18]

From the many nominated candidates (1,025 in number) only 874
were approved. Those candidates with incomplete and invalid sets of
documents, i.e., certificates showing no previous convictions, etc., and on
some occasions those persons who were too big a threat to the authorities
were rejected. There were 599 candidates who competed. The largest
number nominated, after the Government were: the BAPU–Vrabtcha 1, the
WP and the BAPU–Pladne. The NSM of Al. Tzankov also put forth a
significant number of candidates.

In eight constituencies no elections were held since there was only
one candidate in each and in such cases, according to the Electoral Decree,

the candidate had only to be proclaimed. These were mainly constituencies situated in the Southern part of the country—the counties of Bourgas, Plovdiv, Sofia and Stara Zagora.

In conditions of arbitrariness, pre–election terror and violation of the Electoral Law, the Government succeeded in winning with 57.75% of the votes and 140 seats in the National Assembly. That ensured an obedient majority, which was very much needed by the Government in order to enact its and the Monarch's politics. It was evident to everyone that difficult and dramatic months were coming. Each unsuspected turn in governmental politics needed reliable Parliamentary support.

The opposition won 42.25% of the votes in the country and twenty mandates, 16 of which were won by the United Front (WP – 10; BAPU–Pladne – 5 and Zveno – 1). The NSM of Tzankov took two, the Democratic Party one, Agrarians one. It was supported most strongly by the electorate in the cities—Sofia, Plovdiv, Varna, etc, where the headquarters of the former political parties were situated and the propaganda was more intense, the population more literate and informed. The working class, which supported the WP, was concentrated there. Very indicative was the case in the capital city, where in all constituencies the opposition won and the Government suffered total failure (less than 20% of the votes). The city of Sofia sent to Parliament four deputies of the WP (Communist Party)—L. Dyukmendjiev, P. Mitev, N. Sakarov and D. Zahariev, two from the NSM (Al. Tzankov and T. Kojuharov) and one from the Democratic Party (N. Mushanov). The most significant success was achieved by the United Front in the county of Bourgas, where it won more than one third of the votes and three deputy seats.[19]

The results of the elections for the Twenty–fifth National Assembly show the correlation of the political powers and their influence in Bulgaria under the recent onset of war conditions. Although not reflecting the actual situation due to the imposed non–party regime, forgeries during the elections and the impossibility of providing a real pre–election campaign, the elections showed the regrouping of the social and political powers that had already taken place in the country.

Of special significance among the reasons for the regrouping was the development in the foreign political situation. The failure of the parties that established the Democratic Union in the prior election to reach an agreement was due to the changes in international conditions. Munich, the

Czechoslovakian tragedy, the German–Russian Pact and the outbreak of the war split the partners of that former pre–election union forever.

The United Front combined the efforts of a close circle of party and political formations. Although they made a lot of tactical mistakes due to the appetites of various partners for individual aggrandizement, most of the opposition deputies were its candidates. The political powers of the democratic–liberal trend achieved modest results and succeeded to sending only one representative to the National Assembly—Nikola Mushanov, leader of the DP.

The two factions in political life in Bulgaria had already moved away. The democratic–liberal's influence was weakening, especially at a time when perspective for a successful orientation towards Great Britain and France was fading away. The revolutionary left–wing faction started on its independent road no longer permitting agreements with the democrats; they mastered the strength and energy for a future decisive role in the ruling of the country.

The former leaders of the political parties orientated to the countries of the Western democracies, repudiated the aggression of Hitler in Austria and the August Pact. The parties that were partners in the United Front that had favored a republic were striving for friendship with the USSR and were inclined to justify the German–Soviet collaboration on the very eve of the war. The war itself, for WP, was simply imperialistic. In this situation, only the ruling powers reaped the dividends. The separating of the two political factions in the struggle against the authoritarian regime meant further strengthening of the positions (although temporary) of the reactionary trend, because neither the United Front nor the democrat–liberals could dominate the life of the country at that time.

Generation of a New Opposition

During the Second World War, the Twenty–fifth National Assembly was in session. Especially after Bulgaria joined the Axis the internal political life in the country became dependent up on world event. The turn in the development of the battle was accompanied by the establishment of a new political coalition, the Fatherland Front (FF), in which the WP, Zveno, the BAPU–Pladne and a part of the BSDP participated.

The first FF–Government, which was established with the incursion of the Soviet army from the northeast, dissolved the National Assembly in the first days of its regime. The revolutionary–left political trend came to power in Bulgaria. The elimination of the opposition was final and as later turned out, irretrievable.

The strongest opposition to the new government arose within the FF. In the period of October–November, 1944 a mood of opposition mainly within the BAPU had emerged. The dissatisfaction was pointed against the attempts of the Communists to dominate the coalition. Decree No.4 of the Council of Ministers, accepted on the initiative of the War Minister Damyan Veltchev, on October 23, 1944, was not directed to the overthrow of the Government of the FF, but it gave cause for a mass action of the Bulgarian Workers' Party (Communists) against the figure around whom the opposition had rallied—G. M. Dimitrov (Gemeto).

The conflict had come to a head gradually and reached its dramatic outcome in 1946-1947. As opposition powers included: a large part of the BAPU together with its leaders, some members of the BSDP and a group of independent intellectuals. They considered the FF a coalition of political partners with an anti-fascist purpose, striving for democratic reforms in the country; they enjoyed the support of the Allied victors and most of all of the USA and Great Britain. Their supporters were the numerous farmers and democratically inclined citizens. The conflict arose due to the strengthening hegemony of the Communists in the FF and the evident efforts of the BWP(c) to dictate the conditions of the coalition to its partners.

In addition, political life was full of tension because the tenaciously defended tactics of the FF (in fact the BWP(c) was reticent character of the formation, with a multi–party system be within the framework of the FF. The curiousness of this situation arose from the fact that, in reality, Bulgaria was continuing to live under a non–party system. Only one party existed: – the Government of the FF supported by a foreign military power which was present in the country. It was the wish of this "party" to hold elections without officially recognized opposition, i.e. without legitimate rivals in the election contest which would simply be a continuation of practice in Bulgaria during the recent years of non–party elections.

After the decisive protests of the opposition and the interference by representatives of the USA and Great Britain in the Allied Control Commission (ACC), the elections which were set for August 25, 1945 were postponed. This was due to the refusal by both Great Powers to recognize them as democratic and legal. In addition, the successful interference of foreign governments in home affairs was possible because Bulgaria had not as yet signed a peace treaty.

The restoration of the multi-party system was in fact put into place in September 1945, when the opposition groups were "allowed" to register as parties and to publish their newspapers. For a comparatively short period of time the groups which left the FF were registered—an opposition Agrarian Union with Nikola Petkov as its leader and its newspaper *"Narodno Zemedelsko Zname"* ("People's Agrarian Banner"); an opposition BSDP led by Kosta Lultchev and a party newspaper called *"Svoboden Narod"* ("Free People"). The Democratic Party led by Nikola Mushanov was restored as was the party newspaper *"Zname"* ("Banner"). The Radical Party headed, by St. Kosturkov and its newspaper *"Radical"* appeared again, but on September 20, 1945 it joined the FF. The right-wing Radicals split from the RP with their newspaper own *"Naroden Glas"* ("People's Voice") in support of the opposition. Only the Liberals were not permitted to have a legal organization owing to their Germanophile past. In this way the multi-party political system was restored. The parties were striving for wider support and trust among the people by the use of propaganda and organizational activity. Political life became more dynamic and offered (at least formally) possibilities for alternative decisions.

The Difficult Tactics of Boycott

On September 11, 1945 the Council of Ministers accepted a Decree for changing the Decree regulating the election of deputies to the National Assembly. Two decrees of the Regency—No.211 and No.212—were published in *"Darjaven Vestnik"* ("Official Gazette").[20] The changes concerned mainly the requirements for the electors and the participation of the parties in the elections. The new stipulations were that the right to vote was given to all persons, male or female, over 19 years of age, having civil rights according to the meaning of Article 8 of the Constitution. To be elected persons of both sexes must be over 23 years of age who had no fascist affiliations in their past (Article 38). Servicemen could also vote; voting was not obligatory. Political parties, registered in the term required by the Decree, solely or as a coalition, but on one ballot-paper could participate in the elections.

The opposition stood categorically against the Electoral Law, de-claring it unconstitutional. In the opposition party newspapers requests for changes appeared—the militia, servicemen and forest guards should not be permitted to vote; the candidates for deputies must be over 30 years of age and their inviolability be guaranteed. Obligatory voting and the right to put oneself forward as a candidate in more than one constituency was requested.[21]

According to the opposition not only were the age restrictions for electors and those elected unconstitutional, so was voting by the military. In this way those in power ensured for themselves thousands of votes; the withdrawal of a deputy at the request of his party because he had betrayed its ideas and discipline; the counting of ballot-papers with signs and marks as being legitimate, which would be a gross violation of the secrecy of voting.

On October 16, 1945 the opposition powers published an Appeal to the Bulgarian people, announcing their decision not to take part in the elections and calling upon the citizens to boycott the election.[22] A series of reasons were given: the unconstitutional substance of the Electoral Law, personal liberty was not guaranteed—throughout the country the armed militia was in the hands of the Communists, acts of violence and repression were common; the fascist Law for Protection of the State was replaced by the Law for Protection of People's Power; clubs were dissolved, meetings were prohibited; the Ministry for Internal Affairs and Ministry for Foreign Affairs were in the hands of one party, which established in the country a one-party power and engaged in unprecedented terror and the denial of the Government to allow the opposition to use the radio. The appeal was signed by the BAPU, BSDP and the independent intellectuals.

The term for declaring candidacies expired on 18th of October. Only the National Committee (NC) of the FF had registered. There appeared some reports in the press of opposition candidates in the constituencies of Dryanovo, the city of Sofia and Vratza. The fears of some people that Gitchev's men would take advantage of the FF-opposition boycott of the FF and people's dissatisfaction putting forward candidates turned out to be unjustified. Furthermore, on November 10, 1945 a treaty for unity of the agrarian powers was signed by Nikola Petkov and Dimitar Gitchev.

The DP also announced its decision not to take part in the elections. It strictly kept its line of opposition to the FF, considering it as a "state party, which by theory and practice exists in the totalitarian state".[23] The Democrats also proclaimed themselves against the new Electoral Law, considering it unconstitutional, giving the opportunity to one party to determine the behavior of the deputies in the Parliament.

The DP was pursuing its goal zealously—democratic changes in the country, but based on the Turnovo Constitution, restoration of Parliamentary practice, normal party life without the dominating role of the FF and most of all of the BWP(c), foreign policy directed toward friendship with Great Britain and the USA. Its attempts to establish a broad oppositional coalition against the FF was unsuccessful both then and a year later in the elections for Grand National Assembly. Without the ability chance to reach an official agreement, the DP in each case was allied in the acts of the FF–opposition. This was the reason for the response written by Tzveti Ivanov and published on the pages of "*Svoboden Narod*" against the attacks of some representatives of the BWP(c) on the relationship between the FF–opposition and the DP. Calling them to look closely into the ranks of their own ruling coalition, he claimed: "There was and there always will be reaction in Bulgaria. Its decisive offensive started on May 19, 1934. Prime–Minister of Bulgaria at that time was Mr. Kimon Georgiev, too."[24]

Until the last moment the opposition was trying to postpone the elections for the Twenty–sixth National Assembly. On the 14th of November Kr. Pastuhov, N. Petkov, K. Lultchev and P. Stoyanov visited the regents with a request for postponing of the Parliamentary elections because of the unequal conditions for preparation and propaganda. A verbal note was sent by the American Government to the Prime Minister of Bulgaria, signed by the USA representative in Bulgaria Meynard Barns, stating that the Government elected in this way would not be representative. These requests of the opposition and the USA had no effect.

The FF preparation for the election was feverish and obstinate. For the first time the coalition would represent itself on Parliamentary elections and its political prestige in the country and abroad depended on this presentation. According to the new Electoral Law one deputy had to be elected to represent 20,000 citizens—in this way the number of seats was established at 220. The complicated relations between the parties in the FF itself and their appetites for more mandates contributed to the election of 276 deputies (by 56 more), which in fact was a diversion from the law. The quotas were determined for the ruling parties in the FF ballot–papers (for the BWP and the BAPU – 94 each; for the PC "Zveno" – 45; for BSDP – 31 and for the Radicals – 11). This was not the real correlation, but the

BWP(c) needed as wide as possible party representation in the Parliament, even if it was only by participation in the FF.

On October 12th and 13th a central course for FF pre-election campaign propagandists from all over the country was organized in Sofia. With a huge meeting held on October 19th the NC of the FF opened the pre-election campaign. The Central Election Committee summoned writers, actors and artists to help prepare the pre-election propaganda. In the beginning of November, 1945 Georgi Dimitrov returned from Moscow after long years of working in the Communist International. It was on the initiative of the NC of the FF that a Central commission for public control of the elections was established with as Prof. St. Balamezov as its president.[25]

Included in the FF pre-election platform were promises for signing a just and honorable peace treaty, for friendship with the USSR and all liberty-loving peoples, the complete destruction of all remnants of fascism, for further development of democratization in all spheres of life and broad economic initiatives. Slogans were raised against the tactics of boycott of the opposition. A threatening slogan written with large letters appeared on the central building of the Bulgarian Agrarian Cooperative Bank: "The one who does not vote on the 18th of November, is an enemy and traitor to the Bulgarian people!" The active appeal in the countryside was: "To win the village for the Fatherland Front!"; with the assistance of the labor-culture brigades, meetings were organized to guarantee 100% participation by the villagers.[26]

The opposition, still not well-organized in the short period after its registration, was appealing for a boycott. The most persistent propaganda was in full swing in the county of Pleven, where the influence of the Agrarian leaders G. M. Dimitrov and N. Petkov was very strong. The same hectic activity could be observed in the region of Pazardjik. The opposition there had greater influence in the villages, almost the entire YAU (Young Agrarian Union) and the agrarian intelligentsia were with the opposition, the town organizations of the FF, in the majority, supported it as well. The correlation of the agrarian forces for the county of Pazardjik was: 25% with G.M. Dimitrov, 25%—with the FF and 50% with varying positions.[27]

The elections on November 18, 1945 were held with the relatively active participation of the electorate. Furthermore, according to the new Electoral Law, voting was not compulsory. Also, under the Law 771,283 more Bulgarian citizens were given the right to vote in comparison with the elections of 1939/40. These were men between 19 and 21 years of age and servicemen. For women, the number of those permitted to vote was considerably extended—by 1,009,149. This number involved the women between 19 and 21 and those who were unmarried.

In fact, this time almost the same percentage of men voted even though the Law stated voting was not obligatory. With the women who voted we can observe a considerable increase in political activity—82.2% in 1945 as compared to 45.8% in 1939/40. In both cases voting was not an obligation for them, it was by choice. While in all counties of Bulgaria women voted much more actively in 1945, it was not the case with the men. In the counties of Plovdiv, Sofia, Stara Zagora and Pleven the percentage of men who voted was lower in comparison with the former elections. Again, as in 1939/40, the population in the villages voted more actively than in towns (the average for the country was 85.8% and 82.6% respectively). Almost equal was the activity of the electors in towns and villages in the counties of Bourgas and Pleven only.[28]

The total results for the country showed electoral participation of 85.2%. 88.3% of these voted for the FF. The remaining almost 12% obviously did not support the Government, but were afraid not to vote, even though according to the law voting was a matter of choice. If to the number of those who had not voted (had boycotted the elections) we add the number of those, who on the 18th of November, did not vote for the FF (who, in fact, supported the opposition), we can see that almost one fourth (24.76%) of the Bulgarian electorate declared themselves against the Government. Among the different regions the strongest opposition was in the county of Rousse (37.33%), Pleven (29.64%) and Sofia (25.81%). In Tchirpan, Rousse and Razgrad the FF registered its weakest support, while in Kotel, Karnobat and Tzarevo it received the indisputable support of over 94% of the votes.[29]

The invalid ballot-papers were white. Some also voted with newspaper cuttings, empty envelopes, slogans against the FF, with the picture of N. Petkov or slogans with his name on them. The servicemen cast their ballots in the regiments, which strengthened the possibility of control over their participation. 97.5% of them took part in the elections, 92% of those voted for the FF. What makes an impression is the fact that the number of invalid ballot-papers was bigger in those places where more military voted, in the army airports and in the Military School in Sofia.[30]

The opposition rejected the results of the elections as untrue and falsified, achieved in an atmosphere of arbitrariness and chilling fear, held throughout the country with only one ballot-paper and in a contest without any political opponents. Days after the elections in Sofia the official publication of the results could not be prepared. According to the "*Svoboden narod*" newspaper, the results in Rousse and Plovdiv had shown that the working class had begun to withdraw from the FF. The DP declared that the elections could not be considered legitimate, because the FF, by law and practice in the present FF-state, was not simple governmental political group, but a state institution with all the attributes of the state power.[31]

The FF parties evaluated highly the election results. Citing "the slanderous" campaign of the opposition, they declared that in practice their opponent took part in the election contest, calling upon the electors to boycott. For them the battle was enjoined and they were the indisputable winners.[32]

In his speech on Radio Sofia on November 22, 1945 the Minister of Internal Affairs, Anton Yugov, emphasized that for the first time in Bulgarian political history free elections were held; that never before had so many electors participated and voted for one political power at the same time. According to him, the results from the elections had shown that the boycott by the opposition failed catastrophically; that with the election victory the Bulgarian people and mainly the Bulgarians in the villages had shown they stood firmly behind the FF; that the results would put an end to many of the doubts and the accusations that a minority was ruling Bulgaria and that the Government is not representative or without the backing of the majority of the people.[33]

In November, 1945 the majority of the Bulgarian electors supported the ruling union of FF-parties. This was a real expression of the desire of the people after the war for changes and for democratization of society. They had believed the FF Government; that this was the new route they would take; that they were the hope of post-war Bulgaria for a peaceful and reasonable future. It is not surprising that most voters had supported the ruling coalition, in which the leading role was played by a party that had never before ruled the country.

The powers of the opposition, soon registered as parties, could not organize in the short term before the election day. Among the FF parties ambivalent feelings continued. For the general elector it was still not clear what had changed in the short space of one year among the ranks of the ruling coalition. For him to vote in favor of the FF meant to vote for the new, for change, for the defeat of fascism, for choosing the side of the allies. The opposition had not had enough time to persuade and propagandize, to prove the one–party character of the regime. Using its excellent network of its functioning party committees throughout the country, the Communist Party was now in charge of the Ministry of Interior and the People's Militia. It held almost all the local administration posts and some positions in the supreme bodies of the State authorities. Having all this in mind, the opposition chose the tactic of boycott, hoping for cooperation from the Allied Control Commission. At this moment of determination for renovation and action, the boycott, a very difficult tactic, could hardly be successful even from a psychological point of view. In spite of everything, almost 25% of the electorate did not support the FF—an impressive number. Some strata of the city populations as well as of the farmers stood vigorously behind the opposition. The result foretold a dramatic political struggle, which would for the most part take place outside of Parliament.

Second Referendum. Monarchy or Republic?

On August 16, 1946 the political campaign for a referendum to decide the future form of government in Bulgaria began. Even today arguments for the legal grounds of this plebiscite exist, because the Turnovo Constitution did not provide for such a form of referendum. The results were needed before the decisive elections for the Grand National Assembly. The aim of the FF was not only to introduce alterations in the Turnovo Constitution (the form of government—monarchy—to be replaced with a republican one), but to draw up and pass on a new Constitution.

For the carrying out of the referendum, a Central Committee was established with representatives from the five ruling parties and from the mass public organizations. A wide propaganda campaign launched in favor of the idea of a Republic. Large scale meetings were organized by the Parent–Teachers Union and the Barristers and Doctors unions. In Sofia, a huge meeting was called by the Organization of the Central Jewish Committee of the FF, calling upon all Jews in Bulgaria to vote for the People's Republic. A speech was delivered by Jaques Nathan. Two hundred thousand attended a meeting organized by the City and County Committees of the BWP(c) which was held on the square in front of the National Bank in Sofia. On September 1, 1946 in Rousse, a county convention of the Turks was organized. It was stated at the convention that in two years under a republican government "the Turks in Bulgaria will have their own people's intelligentsia". Thousands of resolutions from meetings and gatherings were addressed to the capital city. On the 4th of September in the King's Palace a documentary and well-illustrated exhibition against the monarchy was opened. It was visited with curiosity by many citizens.[34]

Actually, nobody in Bulgaria was agitating, at least open, in favor of the monarchy. All existing parties—in the FF and out of it (even the Democratic Party)—supported the idea of a republic. The BWP(c) came forward with an appeal to the Bulgarian people in which it was stated that the dynasty of the Coburgs was a faithful agency of German imperialism. The slogan was: "Never more monarchy! Never more fascism!".[35]

Despite the united position of the legitimate political parties, the struggle with the opposition continued, although all—both ruling and opposition parties—were appealing to the voters to mark the ballot-paper for the republic. The participants in the referendum were called upon to vote in favor of a republic, but they had to figure out who was more sincerely republican—the FF or the opposition.

On August 31, 1946 the "Rabotnitchesko Delo" newspaper ("Worker's Cause") came out with an editorial "Under republican masks of the reactionary opposition". It said: "The followers of N. Petkov and Pastuhov are allied with King's Democrats in the camp of the reactionaries. The masks of these false republicans have to be removed... We consider, that the oppositionist groups do not have the right to present themselves as defenders of the Turnovo Constitution... There is a need not only to abolish the monarchy, but also to ensure the power for the people, to cut the roots of the reactionaries".

The slogan of the opposition was: "The Turnovo Constitution without monarchy!". For the Agrarians, "republic" meant power to the people. They were proud that the BAPU had been the first to bring into existence the republic.[36] The opposition press as a whole noted that the referendum would solve only the problem of the kind of the government in this country. The stress had to be put not upon the plebiscite, but on the choice of deputies for the Grand National Assembly. It had to determine what the character of the republic would be.

The referendum of September 8, 1946 marked an even higher degree of political activity in the country. More than 4,000,000 voters went to the polls registering a participation of 91.67%. The counties of Gorna

Djumaya, Bourgas and Vratza were most active (over 94%)—they had been the leaders in participation one year ago, in the elections for the Twenty-sixth National Assembly. The same was true of the counties with the weakest participation; the counties of Pleven and Rousse were again the most passive. In their case it was not only a problem of the number of votes. The counties with highest percentage of participation in the referendum were "the most republican". In the county of Gorna Djumaya 94.02% of all electors voted for the republic.[37]

In contrast, the counties with the smallest participation had, comparatively, the lowest percentage in support of the republic. What was more, on November 18, 1945, the counties of Rousse and Pleven showed the least support for the ruling FF by applying the tactic of boycott. In the city of Rousse, those were 67.18% of the voters who supported the republic. These results were not unexpected. The days immediately following September 9, 1944, in Rousse proved to be extremely difficult for the newly established authority. The strong disposition against the ruling union determined the electoral behavior of the citizens in this region, regardless of the fact that in the case of the referendum, the opposition parties also called upon their adherents to vote for the republic. Many representatives of the intelligentsia in the city had agitated in favor of the crown. On the day of the referendum, a large percentage of the teachers who were chairmen of the polling stations "manifested themselves as reactionaries and partisans of the monarchy". As a result, the FF County Committee fired at least three or four men from each district; as late as September 30, 1946, lists with the names of these men and separate lists of the names of the teachers with pro-fascist backgrounds had to be prepared.[38]

About 85% of the participants in the referendum supported the republic. 4.24% of the voters dared to vote for monarchy. Some chose to take part with slogans and other invalid ballot-papers, obviously feeling frightened that the secrecy of the vote would be violated. The results defended the idea of a republic without regard for the different views held by the FF and the opposition regarding what a republic should be. The regions where there was a strong opposition to the FF were identified; as were those which most strongly supported the government party. Uncertainties remained in the places where the people were able to vote freely in favor of the opposition in accordance with their convictions.

The Dark Red Ballot-Paper

The offensive of the FF against the opposition on the eve of the elections for the Sixth Grand National Assembly put a severe strain on political life. Under the pretext of quelling a possible attempt for a coup d'etat, the BWP(c) undertook measures to strengthen its political role in the life of the country. As early as the summer of 1946 it took control of the army, by dismissing from service 1,930 officers and the Minister of War. An armed workers' militia was established with units placed in each town and in industrial enterprises. Some of the leaders of the opposition—Kr. Pastuhov and Dr. G. M. Dimitrov—were brought to trial; publication of opposition newspapers was halted. The FF committees purged all "reactionary" elements who appeared to be reluctant when it came to supporting the government of the FF. The Twenty–sixth National Assembly passed some economic laws which infringed upon the rights and interests of the private sector.

The BWP(c) strengthened its lead position in the FF, the committees were composed of 55.7% Communists, 31.4% Agrarians, 3% Social–Democrats, 1.3% from "Zveno" and 8.6% with no party affiliation. At the Tenth Plenum of the BWP held in 1946, decision to participate in the forthcoming elections for a Constitutional Assembly was made. This time the Communist Party wanted one FF ballot–paper, not to be based on the party principle, but upon "the actual influence of each political power". Having occupied key positions in the life of Bulgaria, the BWP(c) insisted that it should have the majority of the candidates listed on the ballot–papers be from their party. This was the price of its participation. The mechanism to be used was ballot–papers with the same list of FF candidates, but in different colors to be chosen by supporters of the various FF parties thus expressing their political preference. Georgi Dimitrov's statement on the issue was indicative: "If this proposal of ours is not accepted, then the BWP(c) will come out independently, and independently in such a way, that wood and stone will sense the might and influence of our party."[39]

Under the conditions of the agreement for FF collaboration in the elections, published on September 29, 1946, the FF parties committed themselves to collaborate and fight for unity of the organization; to expose the character of the opposition against the people; to come out with an election platform, a substantial part of which had to be worked out jointly and to draw up a new Constitution, to be published later in "*Rabotnitchesko Delo*".

This project kindled an intense pre–electoral struggle. The entire opposition proclaimed itself against it, calling it "Communist Party statutes". Petkov's supporters proclaimed the project unacceptable saying, that private property was not guaranteed, inheritance, residence, even the Constitution itself could be altered when the authorities wished without summoning a Grand National Assembly.[40] What was more, this project was intended to give "Constitutional sanctions to the entire political, economic, social, legislative and social–party activity of the Fatherland Front regime after September 9, 1944". The division of power was eliminated, the National Assembly concentrated all powers in its hands and ruled both the legislative and executive branches of the government.[41]

It seemed that the danger of the electorate being influenced by the statute rejecting private property was a real one, because on the 27th of October, election day, the "*Otetchestven Front*" ("Fatherland Front") newspaper printed a letter of explanation written by K. Georgiev and G. Dimitrov. It read: "In the Grand National Assembly we shall offer Article 8 of the project for the Constitution to enact clearly and unequivocally the private property rights of the farmer, of the peasant, of the craftsman, of the people of manual labor and mental work, and the right to inherit this private property will be fixed and guaranteed for its owners and their successors for ever".[42]

The opposition powers wanted the parliamentary elections postponed because of a shortage of time for organization and the lack of the requested prerequisites: insurance of freedom of speech and of the press as well as of pre–election propaganda. Examples of violations of the Electoral Law were stated, which envisaged a two–month period for organization of the elections. At the same time, many members of the Permanent Committee (PC) of BAPU, of the Secretariat of AYU, of BSDP and of the Social–Democratic Youth were languishing in concentration camps and prisons.[43] In spite of the protests the date remained the same.

In a resolution of the Supreme Party Council, dated the 15th of September, the Democratic Party came out with an appeal for unity of all opposition forces in the elections for the GNA. The FF–opposition refused to join hands with the Democrats for a variety of reasons: the DP rejected entirely the FF, its program and its actions of the 9th of September; the DP had been rejecting the FF even before the 9th of September; the BAPU had never put its party interests above those of the people, it had always received the power from the people even during the reign of Boris; the sharp division of the Bulgarian interests was not in the interest of the Bulgarian people.[44] The Democrats were convinced that the struggle against the FF and its policies was a necessity for the country and the people, and that the people could not expect much from men who were still arguing among themselves about who had been responsible for the actions on the 9th of September. [45]

The DP took part in the pre-election campaign with their own platform in which they urged restoration of democracy in the form of a bourgeois parliamentary republic. The basic aspects of the Project of the Democrats for a Constitution were: defense of private property and initiative, civil liberties, a Constitutional court and the division of powers. This party declared explicitly, that it had no part in the events of September 9, 1944 and the actions of the FF-parties after this date. The appeal was addressed to all who were discontented with the FF, who were affected by the 9th of September and the economic measures of the Government and the Twenty-sixth National Assembly.[46]

The RDP(u) also came out with a declaration. It summoned the Radicals to reach agreement on candidates to share the ballot-papers with the progressive-democratic parties in those places where it was possible win votes. If such an agreement could not be reached, they were urged to vote only for candidates of those progressive-democratic parties with proven merit and "well-tried leaders in the struggle for the victory of Bulgarian democracy."[47]

The FF-opposition stood for peace and friendship with the great powers; for a free, independent, prosperous, people's, republic; for complete liberty; for the reorganization of the militia from a party into a state body; for county autonomy; for non-interference in the private economic life of Bulgarian citizens; for an FF as it was established before September 9, 1944; for the Turnovo Constitution without the articles in favor of a monarchy. In spite of the unfulfilled wish that elections be postponed, this time the opposition decided to participate in the electoral contest. It addressed its appeal to all the population—both in the villages and in the towns—to support it in its efforts to ensure a democratic future for Bulgaria.

The pre-election campaign was dramatic in nature and politically uncompromising. According to the semi-official *"Rabotnitcesko Delo"* and *"Otetchestwen Front"* newspapers the campaigning went smoothly, in an atmosphere of freedom of speech and expression. The opposition news-papers from that time are filled with reports of protests organized to disrupt pre-election meetings, attacks and the breaking of meetings, inactivity by the militia and beatings. Long lists with the names of opposition candidates, interned or sent to prisons were published.

There was great uncertainty among the members of the People's Union "Zveno". In the counties of Rousse, Pleven, Varna, Plovdiv and in the city of Sofia many of the organizations of the BAPU, the BSDP and the PU "Zveno" split and deserted to the opposition. The Fatherland Front committees collapsed in Turnovo and the region where there was strong anti-communist sentiment.

On the 19th of October a massive pre-election meeting of the opposition was held on "9th of September" Square in front of the National Bank. The citizens of Sofia carried slogans, which read "Down with the Communist dictatorship!" and "Vote with the white ballot-paper on the 27th towards liberty!". Many peasants from the neighboring villages came to the meeting by carts. Pre-election speeches were delivered by N. Petkov, K. Lultchev, Prof. P. Styanov, A. Stamboliiski, Dr. At. Moskov. Regardless of the threats made by the government, there gathered a huge mass of people, who believed in victory. Later the FF-press called them "former fascists, bits of fluff and dandies, citizens with unearned income".[48] Immediately before the election day the opposition appealed to the Jews to vote with the white ballot-paper, against racial prejudice, for autonomy of the Jewish counties and the right to freely immigrate abroad. The citizens from the Pirin region and Macedonian immigrants were also approached on this occasion, but in their case by an appeal from the BWP(c) urging them to vote with the dark red ballot-paper.[49]

A huge meeting was held by the Fatherland Front parties on the 25th of October in Sofia. About 200,000 citizens were present on the square, where the main speaker was Georgi Dimitrov. One last appeal was addressed for support of the FF against "the reactionary" opposition.

The election on October 27, 1946 was held with voter participation reaching unprecedented level. What is most impressive is the almost equal participation of men and women, which was due, as in 1945, mainly to the sharp increase of the political activity of women (in the county of Bourgas – 95.5%), rather than to the slight increase of the percentage of men who voted. In general, the population in the counties of Bourgas and Stara Zagora had been the most active, comparatively less in the regions of Sofia and Plovdiv. The already established tendency for a larger number of votes in the village counties, than in the city was preserved. This was characteristic, without exception, of all counties.[50]

The results of the elections show an overwhelming and significant victory for the Fatherland Front and, most of all, for its dominant party, the BWP(c). It had a superior result in most of the villages and towns. In the cities it was supported by 57.3% of the vote, and in the villages by 53.2%. This party was an indisputable power in the counties of Plovdiv and Bourgas (60.6% and 59%); its weakest support was in Rousse and Pleven (43.6% and 47.8% respectively). In some counties the candidates of the opposition got more votes than the Communists—Preslav, Rousse, Razgrad, Provadiya, Elena, Veliko Turnovo, Belene. There were villages in the regions of Dupnitza, Kyustendil, Vidin, Gorna Oryachovotza, Varna, etc. where the BAPU and the PU "Zveno" in union with the opposition groups acted against the BWP(c).[51]

In the country the FF received about 70% of the vote. Second after the Communist Party in the ranks of the FF turned out to be the BAPU–Obbov, with its strongest influence in the county of Gorna Djumaya, where it contributed actively to the success of the ruling coalition. The BAPU–Obbov country–wide lost the battle with the other Agrarian formation, the opposition party of N. Petkov. For the PU "Zveno", the BSDP and the Radical Party the results were an utter failure. Their adherents were very few and only their participation in a common ballot–paper gave them seats in the Grand National Assembly.

The opposition registered a considerable success in spite of the pre–election restrictions and arbitrariness: its newspapers were hindered, meetings were disrupted. A substantial number of its candidates, were up to the last moment, in camps and prisons; it had no access to the Bulgarian National Radio. The FF–opposition, the Democratic Party and the invalid ballot–papers (probably used mostly out of fear) received about 30% of the vote.[52] The comparison with the nearly 25% of voters who did not support the FF in the elections for the Twenty–sixth National Assembly shows that the opposition had increased its influence by a small percentage. It was supported most resolutely in the counties that had most actively boycotted the former parliamentary elections—Rousse and Pleven.[53] The vote there had been the strongest against the republic two months ago, even without considering the appeal of the opposition parties. Therefore in these two counties, especially in Rousse there were strong feelings against everything, the initiative for which arose from the policies of the FF and most of all from the BWP(c). If we turn back in time we will find proof for this thesis. The county of Rousse was the region where the Communist Party was least popular in nearly every parliamentary election, even while being in opposition.

The weakest support for the FF–opposition was given by the county of Gorna Djumaya.[54] The popularity of the BAPU and the FF in the region of Gorna Djumaya was twice as high as that in the other counties in the country; thus it was here that the FF–opposition was weakest. This exception to the general rule would not seem so strange, if one keeps in mind the strong position of the Agrarian movement there as early as the elections in 1939/40, the tradition in this region to vote for the ruling party and the measures taken by the BWP(c) against the opposition in the county in the days immediately following September 9, 1944.

For the DP the result was more than shattering. It only succeeded in getting more votes compared to the RDP in the FF, but unlike the RDP, it did not win a single seat. Only in the city of Sofia were the Democrats still popular and ranked as the second political power after the BWP(c). This was due mainly to the traditional support of the population in the capital for the Democratic Party, whose leaders lived and worked for many years in Sofia. Big business still supported the former state system and was partial to the Democrats.

The balance achieved from the elections for the Sixth Grand National Assembly was different for the various political powers. For those already in power these were honest elections, in which the people had had their say. According to them, those who voted for the opposition were capitalists, profiteers, reactionaries, pro–fascist elements, collaborators with the Germans in robbing Bulgaria on the one hand and people filled with fear on the other.[55] The FF would continue to rule the country. G. Dimitrov wrote in "*Rabotnitchesko Delo*": "In this respect it (the FF) received once again the necessary parliamentary grounds. The elections themselves showed clearly that in our country no other ruling is possible than the ruling of the FF."[56]

As early as election day, there appeared in the opposition press reports of bloody day of terror against the adherents of the FF–opposition. Shortly after the 27th of October no cables or telephone messages could be received in the offices of the "*Svoboden Narod*" newspaper. A black paper appeared listing those Agrarians and white ballot–paper sympathizers who had been beaten or assassinated. Pictures of many of the victims were published. The conclusion was that the elections had been totally discredited, and that the terror continued after election day. Reprisals were taken in the regions of Pleven, Rousse, Elena, Plovdiv, Dupnitza and elsewhere. In Rousse there was a symbolic burning of the Turnovo Constitution.[57] For the DP the elections proved that "in fact the FF already does not exist as a coalition. It is nothing more than the BWP. It was like this before and especially from now on, it will be like this."[58]

The success of the FF in the elections was sufficient for the coalition to hold a substantial majority in the Parliament and to impose its will in the composition of the new Constitution of the Republic. Only the Parliamentary group of the BWP(c) had more than 59% of the seats. This fact determined the character of the future basic Law and the end of the political struggle between the parliamentary and non–parliamentary opposition.

A significant part of the electorate (64.7%) supported the FF in the hope of a change, a new life and democratization of the country after the war. They relied on the new authority and did not understand completely the split in the FF. They did not support the Democratic Party, seeing it as a symbol of former regimes or were afraid of violence and repression. The vast majority of the Turkish population in the counties of Kardjalii, Turnovo, Omurtag, Shumen, Isperich, Kubrat and Dulovo and the Bulgarian Mohammedans in the Rhodope Mountains voted for the FF candidates.[59] It was the same in the region of Gorna Djumaya.

The intense struggle and the admitted violations during the campaign and the manners in which the election was carried out prevented many electors from voting according to their will, particularly in those places where the opposition leaders had strong influence. Nevertheless, the FF–opposition succeeded in winning 101 places and in the beginning took an active part in the parliamentary discussions, but without the ability to influence the decisions. It was supported by a wide spectrum of the electorate—farmers, some groups of employees, craftsmen and merchants, workers and intelligentsia.

The elections proved that in the future the basic contradiction would be between the BWP(c) and the FF–opposition, the most influential political powers in the country. The remainder of the parties, members of the FF and the non–parliamentary groups, would remain in a position of subjection to this conflict. The victor—BWP(c)—would gradually eliminate the Petkov–Lultchev coalition, the DP and its loyal partners. In the next elections in Bulgaria there would be no opposition at all.

CONCLUSION

I. POLITICAL SYSTEM AND PARLIAMENTARY ELECTIONS

The year 1878 marked both the end of five centuries of foreign domination and the beginning of the restoration of Bulgarian statehood. A new kingdom rose from the antiquated Ottoman Empire hoping to reach its forgotten grandeur again. The Constitution of 1879 was the legislative basis of the new Bulgarian state; it was a considerable legal achievement of modern times and a warranty for democratic parliamentary development. Bulgarians were granted the rights to elect and to be elected without regard to their origin or social status. This was a real challenge for a nation which had until recently been deprived of any political or civil freedoms .

The roots of the two major political trends—the liberal and the conservative—can be traced back to the revival period. A few years after the Liberation these trends developed into the Liberal Party and the National Party. Later, the social structure of Bulgarian society, as a result of the rapid economic growth of the country, served as the basis for the formation of four fractions of the Liberal Party: the National Liberal Party, the Liberal party, the Progressive Liberal Party and the Young Liberal Party. The liberals around P. Karavelov established the Democratic Party. The left-wing parties in this country were also set up at the end of the last century the Bulgarian Labor Social Democratic Party and the Bulgarian Agrarian National Union.

The first years of the twentieth century witnessed only two splits —among the Socialists and the Democrats. These resulted in the establishment of the Radical Democratic Party and the BRSDP (narrow socialists). Generally, the party political system was instituted.

A consolidation process began after the end of the First World War. The liberal parties were the first to unite, as they were burdened with the responsibilities for the unsuccessful and even shameful outcome of the Bulgarian participation in the war. The spreading influence of the Agrarians and the Communists served as a catalyst for the unification of the right-wing political parties—the National Party and the Progressive Liberal Party. Later, the Constitutional Bloc was founded in opposition to the independent

Later, the Constitutional Bloc was founded in opposition to the independent Agrarian government. After a successful coup (in 1923), the right–wing parties founded a governmental party—Democratic *Sgovor*, which was in power for eight years. A new coalition, the National Bloc, consisting of Democrats, National–Liberals, Agrarians and Radical Democrats without the participation of right–wing and left–wing extremes later took power. They did so by means of perfectly legal parliamentary actions.

The 1934 coup marked the beginning of the non–partisan period in Bulgarian history, dated until the end of the Second World War. The coalition Fatherland Front set up a government, dominated by communists and supported by the Russian presence in the country in 1944. The attempt of the opposition to bring back multi–party parliamentary life was unsuccessful. The opposition was decapitated both literally and figuratively and the non–communist parties, which remained in the Fatherland Front, were forced to fuse. Ostensibly, the Agrarian Union within the FF was "preserved", however it did not have any political influence.

In the years after the national Liberation, Bulgarian society forged its leaders—capable and skilful politicians suitable for creating the institutions needed by the new Kingdom. Some were outstanding speakers and excellent politicians. Despite the mistakes they made, they were driven by impatience and the noble purpose to see Bulgaria prosper.

Among the first generation of Bulgarian politicians appear the names of S. Stambolov, P. Karavelov, D. Tsankov, K. Stoilov. New actors came onto the political stage later: N. Tzanov, A. Stamboliyski, D. Blagoev; all leaders of newly established political formations. The prominent politicians from the period between the two world wars were Prof. A. Tsankov, A. Burov, A. Malinov, N. Mushanov, D. Gichev, V. Dimov, S. Kosturkov. The Monarch was becoming more and more influential; on the eve of and during the Second World War he played a decisive role.

The new reality of the war brought forward new heros: G. Dimitrov and V. Kolarov, G. M. Dimitrov and N. Petkov, K. Pastuhov, D. Velchev and K. Georgiev. "Their time" had come and they acted in accordance with their political interests. All of them were republicans and supporters of the anti–fascist coalition. The outcome of their struggle with one another was doomed by the postwar world order.

The existing legal grounds for the establishment of a multiparty political system in Bulgaria provided opportunities for them to participate in the election contests. During the period of the initial formation of political represented various party slogans and platforms. Thus the ruling party was able to explain to the voters who its candidates were and to gain support.

After the introduction of the proportional system, which was supported by most of the parties, the election fight became more relentless and uncompromising. Parties and leaders were praised and condemned by the press, on posters and in appeals, in front of the perplexed voters. However, they preferred this system, where behind the so-called better proportional representation, secret battles for better placement in the party lists were fought. The Agrarians introduced the compulsory vote and made changes in the electoral districts and which, because they were favorable for the rulers, were not abolished later.

The non-partisan system resulted in majority vote. Unofficially, however, the term "governmental candidate", or rather a candidate affiliated to the government was introduced. The effect was a competition between the "party" of the governmental candidacies and the "party" of the non-governmental candidacies (oppositional, or representatives of the old parties).

The restoration of the party system after the end of the war had to meet the requirements of the Allies for democratization of the country and free parliamentary elections. Proportional representation was chosen. Main participants in the election struggle became the Fatherland Front, the Oppositional Fatherland Front and the Democratic Party. Again, party lists determined the candidates and their placement. The pre-election competition became a contest between parties and ideas, rather than between people and their values or lack of them.

There is one other parallel, displaying the complex interactions between the status of the political system and legislation. During the period of non-compulsory voting, and after the introduction of the proportional system, most of the parties took part in the election competitions by themselves. There were only a few coalitions—the "United Opposition" against the Stambolov regime, under the majority vote system; in 1913 the Liberal Bloc under the proportional representation system.

The introduction of the compulsory vote in 1920 marked the increase of coalition participation which continued until 1931 and again after the Second World War. It is obvious, that under the non-compulsory vote, only those who had clear preferences and political orientations cast their ballots. When people were obliged to vote, the political parties preferred to unite in order to attract those who voted only because it was the law. In this case parties which would never have won on their own, gained more votes when participating in coalitions (for example the Bulgarian Social Democratic Party and the Radical Democratic Party participated in the Democratic Sgovor in 1923 and Bulgarian Social Democratic Party and Zveno in the Fatherland Front in 1945).

II. THE BEHAVIOR OF THE VOTERS

Who voted?

The degree of participation of the voters, who sometimes were asked to vote too often, was determined by a number of factors. For example: the inherited attitude towards the state, rooted in the minds of the people during the centuries of domination; some legislative regulations and restrictions; rural or urban, district peculiarities, social status, availability or lack of a communications network, sex. Although they were already living in their own state, Bulgarians were somewhat skeptical or indifferent to the institutions in the years immediately following the Liberation. They were more interested in earning their living and supporting their families than in voting in elections, especially during the harvest seasons. Their unwillingness to participate was strengthened by the behavior of the political parties and their leaders, by the endless fights and ferocious personal attacks. These are some of the reasons why until the end of 19th century, the percentage of voters stayed under 50% and for the first decade of the 20th century was around 50%. In 1914, the percentage of people who actually voted increased substantially due to the atmosphere of insecurity which followed the unsuccessful Balkan wars and the unease about the coming World War.

The Constituent Assembly in the old Bulgarian capital city of Veliko Turnovo recognized each Bulgarian citizen's right to vote. Although this referred only to the male population, the lack of any other electoral restrictions, related to various qualifications (educational, ownership, etc.) provided for mass participation in the elections.

Until 1919 each voter decided for himself whether to go to the polls or not. The compulsory vote was introduced in 1920; this greatly enlarged the number of voters, but not the political activity of the voters. Often the act of voting was considered a boring affliction, even a burden, because of the heavy fines payable as penalty for not voting. In 1945 the voting again became non-compulsory. After the war, people were not obliged to vote by law, however, the participation percentage was extremely high because of the people's hope and desire for change.

This rapid increase in electoral participation can be illustrated by the example of female voting. In 1937 the Election Law regulated the non–compulsory participation of women, but only for widows and married women. The degree of their political response at the parliamentary election in 1938 and 1939/40 was 40–50%. Right after the war all women over 18 years of age, irrespective of their marital status were granted the right to vote. The result was an increase of 80–90%. The Bulgarian women, although not obliged to vote by law, demonstrated higher political response than in 1939/40.

Factors such as literacy, social status, communications and membership in a trade union can not be precisely measured without sociological surveys, which, unfortunately, were not carried out for the periods discussed in this book. It can, however, be concluded that big cities and districts with better systems of communications—Stara Zagora, Turnovo, Kjustendil, Vidin—were more active than others.

The opposite is not always true, however. During this period the percentage of voters in the villages was higher than that of voters in the cities. Often, the people from the villages were forced to vote by the local authorities without having clear motivation due to the lack of information. This was done in the period before the establishment of the Agrarian Union. It was easier for the rulers to force the people living in isolated villages and communities to support them. Good example are the Mustanli and Pashmakli districts.

The non–participation was sometimes used by the opposition as an instrument for protest and disagreement with the politics of the ruling party which made it impossible for voters to freely express themselves. The appeals for boycotts of the elections failed because of the lack of skills in organizing needed for a successful protest. These tactics had been applied in various historical moments out of desperation. The liberals of Stambolov boycotted the 1894 elections after losing the power and the Fatherland Front–opposition, because they did not have time to prepare for the elections. About 15.2% of the voters did not vote in 1945 and this was considered a treachery at that time.

Another form of protest, during the period when voting was compulsory, was the handing in of empty envelopes or invalid ballots. Without ignoring the problem of the political culture of the voters, examples can be given when the number of invalid ballots was suspiciously large. They were either improperly labeled as invalid or contained written words, symbols, names, etc. The elections of 1923 lead the chart of invalid ballots because the number of such ballots, given by supporters of the recently toppled Agrarian government, reached 8.5%. Frequently, the increase in the number of voters was due to social tensions, economic crises or opportunities for change mixed with international prerequisites. The increase in the years 1908, 1914, 1946 was a result of such factors. The economic situation, the unaccomplished national ideal, the social tensions urged the people to make use of their duty and their right to try and change their future by voting.

Motivating Factors

Putting the ballot in the box was in fact the last step of the complex process of election competition. The Bulgarians had to be acquainted with the platforms of the political forces by the press, the radio, the pre–election meetings and posters. Obviously, only the citizens of the big cities had access to these information sources. That is why the opposition had better results in these places. No matter which party was in opposition, it was successful in the administrative and industrial centers having well developed communications. People living in these centers were not so much afraid of political repression and it was harder for the ruling party to terrorize the voters. This situation remained even after the Second World War, when the Communists became dominant in the political life.

The pre–election terror and the lack of information led to the formation of the group of voters always supporting the government. The existence of the compulsory voting law forced a lot of people to vote, despite their unwillingness to do so. It is possible that all these people who had no clear political orientation voted in favor of the ruling party simply to avoid any problems. Most of the voters from Mustanli and Pashmakli districts and some other isolated areas voted for the party in power, no matter which party it was. People in these areas were illiterate, lived without electricity and normal communications and sometimes numbered only 70 or less in a village.

These were poor and underdeveloped regions, and the behavior of their inhabitants was conservative when it came to the possibility of choice. Obviously, poverty could be so severe as to destroy any wish for change and hope for a better life. That is why people from these regions did not support parties, whose platforms stated a radical change—Agrarians, Social Democratic Party and the Communist Party. It seems that the statement "Every country has its South" can find its political example in Bulgaria too.

The region of Petrich was another phenomenon in the Bulgarian South. The unsuccessful attempts to incorporate Macedonia and the Bulgarian population there increased the tension in the Southwestern part of the country. During the rule of the Agrarians these tensions were transformed into hatred and cruelty, because the Government wanted to improve its relations with Yugoslavia. The strong separatist attitudes interfered with the parliamentary elections. Petrich district was the only region in Bulgaria in which a single organization (the Internal Macedonian Revolutionary Organization) dictated the names of the candidates. In the years 1923, 1927 and 1931 no one voted for the Agrarians or their coalitions in that region. In 1927 the local Citizens' list was supported 100%. Petrich became a "state within a state".

Studying the regional results of the different political forces , we can see that they are either traditionally well represented in given regions, or totally unsuccessful. In the first years after the Liberation, people who lived in the home towns and villages of political leaders supported those leaders. In 1884, there were articles in the press describing the "nests" or "strongholds" of the conservatives: Elena, Gorna Oryahovitsa, Tryavna. Later, Vidin became the cradle of the Radical Democrats due to the strong influence of Naicho Tsanov, who was born there. People from Turnovo supported Stambolov and people from Kjustendil—the liberals.

The Democratic party was influential in Sofia and Kjustendil regions.

The Agrarians were successful in Northeast Bulgaria, the regions of Varna, Shumen and Rousse, where riots erupted in 1900 and were suppressed by the rulers. The Agrarians had an excellent network in the region of Pleven, and were traditionally popular among the population of this agrarian region.

From the beginning of their participation in parliamentary elections the Social Democrats "conquered" the regions of Vratsa, Stara Zagora and Turnovo. They were popular there between the wars as well. The "narrow socialists", later communists (since 1927—Labor Party) were supported in the regions of Bourgas and Vidin and on the eve of the Second World War in the regions of Sofia and Gorna Djumaya. Most of their supporters lived in cities with big factories, plants and warehouses. They established trade union organizations which became active in the pre–election struggle. Women from the working class, wives of the workers were also active voters – more active than the rest of the female voters.

The different political parties were traditionally unsuccessful in given regions. For example, people living in the region of Rousse voted against the Communist party. For the whole period discussed in this book, the Communists were unpopular in Rousse. This was especially true in the elections of 1945 and 1946 and the Referendum for Republic of Monarchy when they got the lowest results there. Those whose families had been rich merchants and bankers from the time of the Revival period influenced the lifestyle and political culture of the city. The popularity of the Agrarians in this region was also a factor in the failure of the communists.

Various international events also played an important role in the formation of the vote at different times in Bulgarian electoral history. The first parliamentary elections during the rule of Stambolov (1887) carried the slogan of the National Liberal Party for sustaining the independence and sovereignty of the Kingdom from attacks by Russia. The Conservatives (NP) lost the elections in 1913 because of their Russian orientation and because of the outcome of the Balkan Wars. The failure of the liberal parties in 1919 was due to their foreign policy. According to the judgment of the voters, this foreign policy led the country to catastrophe. The entire Petrich region did not approve the foreign policy of the Agrarians. During the election campaigns in 1939/40 the rulers tolerated some pro–Russian elements because of the recently signed Ribentrop–Molotov Pact. The appeals for everlasting friendship with the peoples from the USSR dominated the propaganda of the Fatherland Front in 1945 and 1946.

Strict preferences and attitudes did not exist among ethnic minorities. There were articles in the press, containing scornful statements concerning the ethnic origin of the group, supporting a given political force. In 1914 the liberal coalition was accused of owing its victory to the votes of the Turks from Gjumurdjina. The Agrarians explained the popularity of the Communists in April 1923 with the support of the Gipsy population. It was often said the Gipsy population was easy to manipulate and could be bribed.

The lack of ethnically based parties freed the vote of the minorities. A separate list was made and used in the elections only in the region of Petrich. Some parties appealed to the refugees from the territories lost in the wars and their organizations in this country—and this was true for the Bulgarian Social Democratic Party. The Radical Democratic Party published its platform in Bulgarian and Turkish for the 1919 elections, hoping to gain the votes of the Turkish population. The Bulgarian Muslims (*pomaks*), living around the Southern border preferred to support the ruling party, no matter which party was ruling. The Jews and the Armenians voted according to their political tastes and social status.

Who Was Elected?

In the first years after the Liberation, the national representation was shaped by a majority election system. This fact provided a vote based on the individual qualities of the candidate—personal values, public respect, and strength of arguments during the election campaign.

Due to the existing electoral system, the results sometimes registered a higher total result for those candidates who did not win a deputy mandate; and the candidates who became members of the National Assembly were supported by less than 50% of the voters (example – 1902, 1911 elections). This was true for the first elections after 1879. Two dates were fixed for the elections and the deputies were elected on the second date, even with only 37–38% of the votes.

After the introduction of the proportional election system, which had the advantage of real representation of the vote, the people's deputies were backed by the votes of the majority of voters. The three influential parties won more than 50% of the votes and thus had more than half of the seats in Parliament. After the changes in the Election Law which were made by the Agrarians in 1923, the percent of deputy seats won by the first political force was considerably higher than the percent of the votes obtained by it in the election.

The voters preferred to cast their ballots for people they knew, who had already been in the Parliament. More than half of the elected deputies were former members of Parliament. It was only in 1908, when the Democratic party won the elections, that the number of newly elected deputies was higher than the number of former members of Parliament. Most of the deputies were Bulgarians. Only 5% were of Turkish ethnic origin. Individual deputies were of Greek, Dalmatian (1901), Croatian

(1899), Cherna Gora (1908) and Pomak (1902) origin. Most of the deputies were between 35 and 45 years of age and had a university education, the majority of them in the field of law. That was why lawyers were the biggest group in the Bulgarian Parliament, followed by the group of merchants. From 1901, after the 1899 establishment of the Agrarian Union, the agrarian lobby increased in the parliamentary hall.

The deputies in the parliament after the Second World War were younger; fewer were university-educated. This was due to the changes in the Election law, which set the age of 23 as a qualification to be elected. The Communist parliamentary group had the lowest level of education. In 1945 women also entered parliament as deputies.

The study of the deputies in the Bulgarian Parliament, collected from elections—free or manipulated—shows that most of the people elected were suitable for their posts. The prevailing group of deputies were lawyers in the age group for creative work which allowed them to participate actively in the formulation and adoption of laws in the years when the bedrock of the state was being constructed.

During the first quarter of the century of their modern history Bulgarians voted in support of the liberal parties. These were the followers of the democratic traditions of the Revival period and symbols of the struggle for national liberation and the unification of the Bulgarians. The period between the two wars gave the voters new challenges—first the crisis pushed the left–wing forces forward and later the right–wing formations took over the parliament and the ministries. After the end of World War II the left–wing forces, dominated by the Communists, won the people's vote. The complete destruction of the opposition was the beginning of a lasting dictatorship, when the vote turned out to be unnecessary.

NOTES

CHAPTER I

1. S. Radev, *Creators of Contemporary Bulgaria*. Sofia, 1911.
2. *Almanac of the Bulgarian Constitution*. Plovdiv, 1911, pp. 107–108.
3. S. Radev, *Creators of Contemporary Bulgaria*. Sofia, 1990, p. 48.
4. *Almanac of the Bulgarian Constitution*. Plovdiv, 1911, p. 126–135.
5. M. Manolova, *Parliamentarism in Bulgaria 1879–1894*. Sofia, 1989, p. 17.
6. P. Milyukov, *The Bulgarian Constitution*. Sofia, 1905.; M. Manolova, *Parliamentarism in Bulgaria 1879–1894*. Sofia, 1989, p. 105.
7. M. Manolova, *Parliamentarism in Bulgaria 1879–1894*. Sofia, 1989, p. 107.
8. *Otetchestvo*, No. 8, April 4, 1884.
9. The picture of the political dispositions in Bulgaria in 1884 was drawn after processing the results of the elections in the different counties, as published in the *"Tarnovska Konstitutsia"* newspaper, No. 45, June 9, 1884; No. 58, July 25, 1884 and No. 66, August 22, 1884.
10. *Otetchestvo*, No. 19, May 16, 1884.
11. *Svoboda*, No. 84, Sept. 16, 1887.
12. *Svoboda*, No 88, Sept. 30, 1887
13. *Svoboda*, No 84, Sept. 16, 1887.
14. *Svoboda*, No 88, Sept. 30, 1887.
15. State Archives – Rousse, f 1k, op. 1, a.e. 223, l. 4.
16. *Narodni prava*, No. 191 and 192, Sept. 12, 1890.
17. *Narodni prava*, No. 184, June 28, 1890.
18. M. Manolova, *Parliamentarism in Bulgaria 1879–1894*. Sofia, 1989, p. 180.
19. State Archives – Rousse, f 1k, op. 1, a. e. 223, l. 3, 9.
20. Ibid., l. 10.
21. *Svoboda*, No. 1469, Sept. 1, 1894.
22. *Svoboda*, No. 1478, Sept. 13, 1894.
23. B. Georgiev, "Formation and initial activity of the Liberal (Radoslavov's) party in Bulgaria (1886–1894)", *Istoritcheski pregled*, 1–2, 1992, p. 113–129.
24. P. Milyukov, *The Bulgarian Constitution*. Sofia, 1905, p. 146; *Svoboda*, No. 1478, Sept. 13, 1894.
25. P. Milyukov, *The Bulgarian Constitution*. Sofia, 1905, pp. 147–148.
26. Ibid., p. 146.

CHAPTER II

1. *Statistical Annual of the Bulgarian Kingdom (SABK)*. 1910, p. 457; see Appendix No. 1.
2. *SABK*, 1910, p. 457; *SABK*, 1933, p. 375.
3. Ibid.
4. *Narodni prava*, No. 39, Apr. 13, 1899.
5. *Narodni prava*, No. 45, May 2, 1899.
6. *Statistics of the Elections for deputies for the Xth National Assembly; SABK*, 1910, p. 457.

7. Evg. Kostov, "General Ratcho Petrov, Life and Professional Career", *Historical Review*, No. 6, 1992, p. 90.

8. *Statistics of the Elections for deputies for the XIth National Assembly*, Sofia, 1903.

9. *Statistics of the Elections for deputies for the XIIth National Assembly*, Sofia, 1904.

10. J. Popov, *The People's Liberal (Stambolov's) Party in Bulgaria 1903–1920*. Sofia, 1986, p. 28.

11. Of Gen. R. Petrov (May 1903 – Oct. 1906, of D. Petkov (Oct. 1906 – Feb. 1907), of D. Stantchov (Feb – March 1907).

12. *Statistics of the Elections for deputies for the XIIIth National Assembly*.

13. *Pryaporetz*, No. 50, Oct. 25, 1903.

14. *Pryaporetz*, No. 62, May 31, 1908; *Statistics of the Elections for deputies for the XIVth National Assembly*, Sofia, 1910.

15. *Pryaporetz*, No. 62, May 31, 1908.

16. Ibid.

17. Ibid.

18. Ibid.

19. Ibid.

20. Ibid., No. 196, Sept. 6, 1911.

21. *Statistics of the Elections for deputies for the XVth National Assembly*, Sofia, 1914.

22. *Pryaporetz*, No. 197, Sept. 8, 1911.

23. Ibid.

24. *SABK*, Sofia, 1913–1922, p. 57.

25. Ibid.

26. Ibid.

27. Ibid., p. 58.

28. Ibid.

29. *Pryaporetz*, No. 40, Feb. 19, 1914.

30. Ibid., No. 46, Feb. 27, 1914.

31. *SABK*, Sofia, 1913–1922, p. 58.

32. Ibid.

CHAPTER III

1. V. Georgiev. *"The foundation of the United People's Progressive Party"*, *Izvestiya na Bulgarskoto Istorichesko Drugestvo*, *(IBID)*, No.33, 1980, p. 111.

2. V. Georgiev. "The 'Entente' bourgeois parties in Bulgaria (1918–1920)". *Godishnik na Sofiiskiya Universitet Istoricheski fakultet (GSU IF)*, No.74, 1983, p. 239.

3. V. Georgiev. "The foundation of the National Liberal Party". *Izvestiya na Bulgarskoto Istorichesko Drugestvo,(IBID)*, 1977, V.30, p. 158.

4. D. Petrova. "The BAPU Program of 1919". *Vekove*, No.2, 1980, p. 40–44.

5. *Radikal*, August 1, 1919.

6. *Mir*, August 11, 1919; Appeal to the Bulgarian citizens, August 15, 1919.

7. V. Georgiev. "The 'Entente' bourgeois parties...", p. 256.

8. *Statistical Annual of the Bulgarian Kingdom*, Sofia, 1933, p. 376–377.

9. *Zemedelsko Zname*, No. 99, August 25, 1919.

10. V. Georgiev. "The 'Entente' bourgeois parties...", p. 268.

11. *Darzaven Vestnik*, No. 264, Febr. 26, 1920.
12. *Darzaven Vestnik*, No. 260, Febr. 21, 1920.
13. *Darzaven Vestnik*, No. 198, Dec. 3, 1919.
14. *Statistical Annual of the Bulgarian Kingdom*, Sofia, 1933, p. 375. Table No.1.
15. M. Koumanov. "To the history of the bourgeois and petty-bourgeois parties in the Kyustendil region (1918-1923)". In *Vutreshnata politika na Bulgaria prez kapitalizma (1879-1944)*. p. 148-149.
16. *Statistical Annual of the Bulgarian Kingdom*, Sofia, 1924. Statistics of the elections for deputies for the Nineteenth National Assembly.
17. V. Georgiev. *The People's Sgovor 1921-1923*. Sofia, 1989, p. 47.
18. *Darzaven Vestnik*, No. 160, October 17, 1922.
19. *Slovo*, November 2 and 15, 1922.
20. *Darzaven Vestnik*, No. 272, March 6, 1923.
21. *Slovo*, No. 303, April 18, 1923.
22. Ibid.
23. *Statistics of the elections for deputies for the Twentieth National Assembly*, Sofia, 1927.
24. *Utro*, No. 4121, April 25, 1923.
25. V. Georgiev. *The People's Sgovor...*, p. 158.
26. *Statistics of the elections for deputies for the Twentieth National Assembly*, Sofia, 1927.
27. *Demokratitcheski Sgovor*, No. 2, October 2, 1923.
28. *Demokratitcheski Sgovor*, No. 5, October 6, 1923.
29. M. Koumanov. "The 9th of June Government and the Parliamentary institute." In: *Bulgaria 1300. Instituzii i durzavni tradizii*, V.3, S., 1983, p. 171.
30. Ibid.
31. *Pryaporetz*, No. 261, November 19, 1923; *Radikal*, No.258, November 16, 1923; *Demokratitcheski Sgovor*, No. 41, November 20, 1923.
32. *Pryaporetz*, No. 261, November 19, 1923.
33. Ibid.
34. G. Danailov. *Studies on the demography of Bulgaria*. Sofia, 1931, p. 215.
35. *Demokratitcheski Sgovor*, No. 42, November 21, 1923. A lesson from the elections.
36. *Statistical Annual of the Bulgarian Kingdom*, 1925,p. 421-423.
37. *Radikal*, No. 262, November 21, 1923.
38. V. Georgiev. "Development of the political system in Bulgaria (1918-1944)". In: *Bulgaria 1300. Instituzii i durzavni tradizii*, 1981, V.1, p. 305.
39. Archive of the Ministry of Internal Affairs, ob-6361, l. 47-47ob.
40. *Zname*, No. 115, May 26, 1927.
41. *Zname*, No. 116, May 27, 1927.
42. *Statistical Annual of the Bulgarian Kingdom*, 1933, p. 376-377.
43. Ibid.
44. Ibid.
45. Ibid.
46. Ibid.
47. *Zname*, No. 118, May 30, 1937.
48. *Pryaporetz*, June 9, 1927.
49. D. Petrova. "The Pre-election Platform of the People's Bloc". in: *Vekove*, No.4, 1975, p. 48-50.

50. *Zname*, No. 134, 135 and 136, June 18th, 19th and 20th, 1931.

51. *Narodni Prava*, No. 40, 42 and 45, June 3rd, 10th and 20th, 1931.

52. Archive of the Ministry of Internal Affairs, ob–4617, 1. 7.

53. *Statistical Annual of the Bulgarian Kingdom*, 1932, p. 370–373.

54. *Narodni Prava*, No. 47, July 1, 1931.

55. *Statistical Annual of the Bulgarian Kingdom*, 1932, p. 370–373.

56. *Mir*, No. 9283, June 22, 1931.

57. Mir, No. 9284, June 23, 1931.

58. V. Georgiev. *Bourgeois and petty-bourgeois parties in Bulgaria 1934-1939*. Sofia, 1971, p. 11, 16, 20 and 28.

CHAPTER IV

1. V. Georgiev. *Bourgeois and petty-bourgeois parties in Bulgaria 1934-1939*, Sofia, 1971, p. 286.

2. Ibid., p. 202–206.

3. *Darjaven vestnik*, No. 234, October 22, 1937.
Darjaven vestnik, No. 3, January 5, 1938.

4. Archives of the Ministry of Internal Affairs (AMVR), ob. 22913, 1. 4; ob. 12928, 1. 106; ob. 804, 1. 19; ob–4125j, 1 8–9.

5. AMVR, ob–1782, t. I, 1. 43.

6. AMVR, ob–21166, t. XII, 1. 54.

7. D. Sirkov. *The election program of the National Front in Bulgaria*. IIIBKP, t. 9, p. 379–380.

8. AMVR, ob–22907, 1. 8; ob–1000, 1. 1.

9. AMVR, ob–23220, 1. 2; ob–1782, t. I, 1. 20, 32.

10. SABK, 1939, p. 730–731.

11. *Zora*, No. 5629, March 28, 1938.

12. SABK, 1939, p. 730–731.

13. Ibid.

14. AMVR, ob–23220, 1. 161.

15. V. Georgiev. *Bourgeois and petty-bourgeois parties in Bulgaria 1934-1939*, Sofia, 1971, pp. 343–344.

16. D. Sirkov, T. Kostadinova. "The results of the elections for the XXVth National Assembly (December 1939 – January 1940)". Statistic data. *Vekove*, 2, 1990, pp. 22–23.

17. The results show, that in some cases the United Front would have had won more seats, if it had submitted only one candidate in the electoral contest.

18. SABK, 1942, p. 776–777.

19. D. Sirkov, T. Kostadinova." The results of the elections...", p. 22–32.

20. *Darjaven vestnik*, No. 214 and 216, September 14 and 17, 1945.

21. *Svoboden narod*, No. 205 and 206, September 18 and 19, 1945.

22. *Narodno zemedelsko zname*, No. 56, October 16, 1945; *Svoboden narod*, No. 229, October 16, 1945.

23. Al. Girginov. "Provide real electoral freedom." *Zname*, No. 2, September 25, 1945.

24. *Svoboden narod*, No. 240, October 28, 1945.

25. *Otetchestven front*, No. 366, November 9, 1945.

26. S. Milanova. "The Parliamentary elections on November 18, 1945 and political life in Bulgaria." *Istoritcheski pregled*, No.7, 1989, p. 38–52.
27. R. Katzarova. "The elections for the XXVIth National Assembly in the Pazardjik region in 1945." *Vekove*, No.5, 1984, p. 70–77.
28. *Statistical Annual of the People's Republic of Bulgaria, 1943–1946*. p. 434–435.
29. *Izgrev*, No. 350, November 21, 1945; *Rabotnitchesko delo*, No. 365, November 22, 1945.
30. M. Isusov. *The political parties in Bulgaria 1944–1948*. Sofia, 1978. p 231.
31. *Zname*, No. 43, December 17, 1945; *Svoboden narod*, No. 262, November 23, 1945.
32. *Izgrev*, No. 350, November 21, 1945.
33. *Rabotnitchesko delo*, No. 366, November 23, 1945.
34. *Rabotnitchesko delo*, No. 197, August 31, 1946.
35. *Rabotnitchesko delo*, No. 198, September 1, 1946.
36. *Narodno zemedelsko zname*, No. 129, September 8, 1946.
37. *Otetchestven front*, No. 636, September 29, 1946;
Rabotnitchesko delo, No. 223, September 29, 1946.
38. DA – Rousse, f. 82, op. 1, a. e. 3, l. 108.
39. *Rabotnitchesko delo*, No. 166, July 27, 1946.
40. *Narodno zemedelsko zname*, No. 156, October 12, 1946.
41. *Zname*, No. 211, October 5, 1946.
42. *Otetchestven front*, No. 560, October 27, 1946.
43. *Narodno zemedelsko zname*, No. 145 and 148, September 29 and October 3, 1946.
44. *Narodno zemedelsko zname*, No. 159, October 9, 1946.
45. *Zname*, No. 222, October 18, 1946.
46. *Zname*, No. 208, October 2, 1946.
47. Ibid.
48. *Svoboden narod*, No. 210, October 20, 1946; Shorthand records of the Sixth GNA, 33rd session, February 4, 1947, p. 513–516.
49. *Svoboden narod*, No. 212 and 213, October 23, and 24, 1946.
50. *Statistical Annual of the People's Republic of Bulgaria, 1947–1948*. p. 316–317.
51. M. Isusov. *The political parties in Bulgaria 1944–1948*. Sofia, 1978. p. 314 and 317.
52. Final reports for the results of the elections for the VIth GNA on October 27, 1946 per counties. *Rabotnitchesko delo*, No. 253, October 31, 1946.
53. Ibid.
54. Ibid.
55. Shorthand records of the Sixth GNA, I regular session, pp. 395–418, 421–465, 508–587.
56. *Rabotnitchesko delo*, October 29, 1946.
57. *Svoboden narod*, No. 220, October 31, 1946.
58. *Zname*, No. 230, October 28, 1946.
59. M. Isusov. *The political parties in Bulgaria 1944–1948*. Sofia, 1978. p. 315.

CHRONOLOGY OF EVENTS

1878, March   The San Stefano Peace Treaty is signed

1878, July   The Berlin Congress

1879, April   The Turnovo Constitution is inaugurated.
                   Universall suffrage provided for all men

1879, September Parliamentary elections for First National Assembly

1880, January   Parliamentary elections for Second National Assembly

1880   The Liberal Party is founded

1881-83   Battenberg's personal regime

1882   Battenberg and the Conservatives introduce voting through
                   delegation

1882   Parliamentary elections for Third National Assembly

1884, May   Parliamentary elections for Fourth National Assembly

1885, September The Bulgarian Principality and Eastern Roumelia unite

1885, October   Serbia starts war against Bulgaria.
                   Bulgaria defends the Union

1886   The King abdicates

1886   The Liberal Party (Radoslavov) and the People's Liberal
                   Party are founded

1887   Ferdinand of Saxe–Coburg–Gotha becomes King of
                   Bulgaria. Stephan Stambolov forms the government

117

1887, September Parliamentary elections for Fifth National Assembly

1890 Parliamentary elections for Sixth National Assembly

1891, August The Bulgarian Social Democratic Party is founded

1893 Parliamentary elections for Seventh National Assembly

1893 The Internal Macedonian–Odrin Revolutionary Organization is founded

1894 The Conservatives come into power. Konstantin Stoilov becomes Prime Minister

1894, September Parliamentary elections for Eighth National Assembly

1895 S. Stambolov is murdered in Sofia

1896 Parliamentary elections for Ninth National Assembly

1896 The Democratic Party is founded

1899 Parliamentary elections for Tenth National Assembly

1901, January Parliamentary elections for Eleventh National Assembly

1902 Parliamentary elections for Twelfth National Assembly

1903 Parliamentary elections for Thirteenth National Assembly Second government of Stambolov's party

1903 The BSDP splits

1903 The anti–Ottoman uprising in Macedonia and Thrace led by the IMRO

1904 The Young Liberal Party is founded

1905 The Radical Democratic Party is founded

1907   Prime Minister D. Petkov is murdered

1908   Parliamentary elections for Fourteenth National Assembly

1908, September Bulgaria proclaims its independence and gives
                    the title of Tsar to Ferdinand

1911, September Parliamentary elections for Fifteenth National Assembly

1912   Introduction of the proportional system

1912–1913   The Balkan wars

1913, November Parliamentary elections for Sixteenth National Assembly

1914, February Parliamentary elections for Seventeenth National Assembly

1914   The First World War staarts

1915   Bulgaria enters the war on the side of Germany

1918   The Entente's attack at Dobro Pole

1918   Ferdinand abdicates in favor of his son Boris

1919   The BWSDP(n.s.) is renamed the Bulgarian Communist
                    Party

1919, August   Parliamentary elections for Eighteenth National Assembly

1919, November The Treaty of Neuilly is signed

1920   Introduction of obligatory voting

1920, March   Parliamentary elections for Nineteenth National Assembly.
                    The Agrarian Union forms a government

1920, November Three Liberal parties unite under the name of National

Liberal Party

1920, December The Conservatives and the Progressive–Liberals unite and found the United People's Progressive Party

1921, October The People's *Sgovor* is established

1922, July The Constitutional Bloc is founded

1922, November Referendum on the wartime Ministers' guilt

1923, April Parliamentary elections for Twentieth National Assembly

1923, June Coup d'Etat. New government led by Prof. Alexander Tzankov

1923, August The Democratic *Sgovor* is founded

1923, September September uprising led by the Communist Party

1923, November Parliamentary elections for Twenty–first National Assembly

1924 The Law on the Defense of the State is passed. The BCP is out of law.

1925, April The Alexander Nevski Cathedral assault

1927 The Bulgarian Workers' Party is founded

1927 Parliamentary elections for Twenty–second National Assembly

1931 The People's Bloc is established by Democrats, Radical Democrats, Agrarians and National Liberals

1931, May Parliamentary elections for Twenty–third National

Assembly. Victory for the oppositional People's Bloc

1934, *May*   Coup d'Etat by the political group "Zveno" and the military. The Parliament is dissolved and political parties are forbidden.

1937, *October*   New Electoral Law is passed. Introduction of majoritarian system. Women get the right to vote.

1938, *March*   Parliamentary elections for Twenty–fourth National Assembly

1939, *December*– Parliamentary elections for Twenty–fifth National
1940, *January*   Assembly

1940, *September* Southern Dobrudja is given back to Bulgaria

1941, *March*   Bulgaria joins the Axis

1941, *April*   The "Marita" operation. Bulgarian troops in Macedonia and Eagan Thrace

1943, *August*   The Fatherland Front is founded

1943, *August*   Tsar Boris dies

1944, *September* A Fatherland Front government is formed. The Red Army is in the country

1945   New opposition emerges from the Fatherland Front

1945, *September* A Decree is promulgated for amendments to the Electoral Law. All males and females over 19 get the right to vote

1945, *November*   Parliamentary elections for Twenty–sixth National Assembly

1946, *September* Referendum for Republic

1946, October   Election for Sixth Grand National Assembly

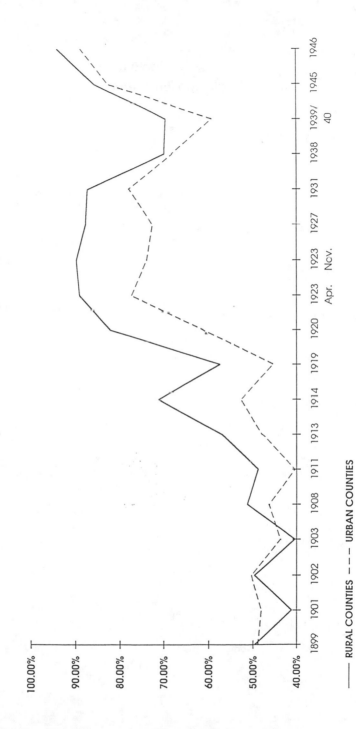

Table No.1

Participation of urban and rural counties

—— RURAL COUNTIES — — — URBAN COUNTIES

Table No.2
Participation of men and women

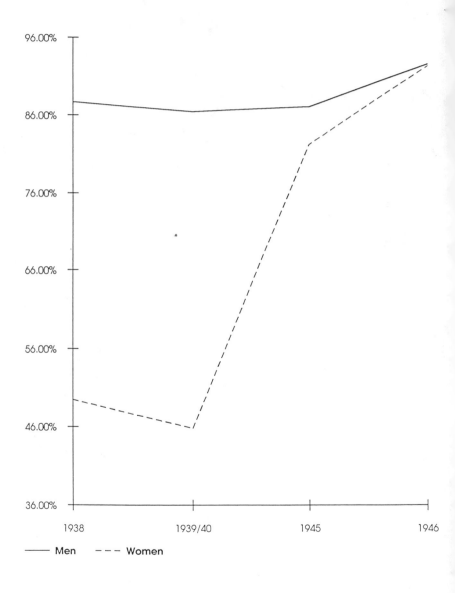